# CARNIVAL!

## 60 RECIPES FOR A BRASILIAN STREET PARTY

# CARNIVAL!

## 60 RECIPES FOR A BRASILIAN STREET PARTY

DAVID PONTE, LIZZY BARBER & JAMIE BARBER

## CABANA
### BRASILIAN BARBECUE

PHOTOGRAPHY BY MARTIN POOLE · ILLUSTRATIONS BY ANITA MANGAN

quadrille

Publishing director: Sarah Lavelle
Creative director: Helen Lewis
Senior editor: Céline Hughes
Original concept, art direction and design: Anita Mangan
Designer on Carnival!: Gemma Hayden
Food photography: Martin Poole
Photograph on pages 112–113: Faith N
All other photography: Jamie Barber,
Matthew Cooper and Josh Ponté in Br
Illustrations: Anita Mangan
Food stylist: Emily Quah
Props stylist: Tamzin Ferdinando
Production: Steve McCabe
Production director: Vincent Smith

First published in 2016 by
Quadrille Publishing
52–54 Southwark Street
London SE1 1UN
www.quadrille.co.uk

Quadrille Publishing in an imprint of F
www.hardiegrant.com.au

ISBN: 978 1 84949 772 5

Printed in China

# CONTENTS

# INTRODUCTION

At Cabana, we love a party. And there's nothing better than taking the party outdoors when the sun is shining and the days are getting longer. It's just another excuse to make a third batch of caipirinhas!

★ ★ ★ ★ ★ ★ ★ ★ ★ ★ ★ ★ ★ ★ ★ ★ ★ ★ ★ ★ ★ ★ ★ ★

Since Brasilian food is all about sharing and getting people together, we know a thing or two about throwing a great party. No matter what the occasion – the Olympics, the football World Cup, the start of summer, your gran's birthday! – there's nothing stopping you from making it the kind of vibrant celebration the Brasilians excel in.

★ ★ ★ ★ ★ ★ ★ ★ ★ ★ ★ ★ ★ ★ ★ ★ ★ ★ ★ ★ ★ ★ ★ ★

We've selected some of our favourite party food for this book, to include little things that are perfect as fingerfood, bigger barbecue feasts, cooling cocktails and ice cream, and everything in between. There's nothing complicated in here – just a whole lot of fun and flavour.

To make things easier, we've suggested a couple of menus: one for a barbecue party (pages 44–45), and one for a street food party (pages 120–121), complete with instructions on what to prepare and when.

★ ★ ★ ★ ★ ★ ★ ★ ★ ★ ★ ★ ★ ★ ★ ★ ★ ★ ★ ★ ★ ★ ★ ★

With a little guidance from us, some extra helping hands, and a few rays, it should be perfectly straightforward to throw a party that will get everyone talking. And hey, if the sun isn't playing ball and the clouds take over, don't despair! Bring the sunshine inside with a couple of our cocktails and get your own samba class started (see pages 88–89).

★ ★ ★ ★ ★ ★ ★ ★ ★ ★ ★ ★ ★ ★ ★ ★ ★ ★ ★ ★ ★ ★ ★ ★

When the last guests have gone and you've swept away those discarded streamers and cocktail swizzler sticks, you'll hopefully have caught the bug for Brasil. The local zest for life is infectious. So check out pages 30–31, get yourself to Rio and have the time of your life!

GET THE
PARTY
STARTED

# BRASILIAN CHICKEN BUCKET

SERVES 4

This Brasilian-style fried chicken is the ultimate dish to enjoy with friends and the futebol. We've taken the traditional Brasilian fried chicken dish *franga passarinho* (which literally means 'chicken in the style of a little bird' because of the bite-sized pieces) and given it added crunch in the form of another well-loved Brasilian ingredient: matchstick potatoes. Best served with a beer in one hand and the remote control in the other.

450g skinless, boneless chicken thighs or breasts
2 garlic cloves, finely crushed
1 onion, finely chopped
2–3 tbsp cheiro verde (equal quantities of chopped flat-leaf parsley and spring onion)
5 tbsp lime juice
125g plain flour
1 tsp baking powder
2 tsp tempero baiano seasoning (page 62)
1 large (about 100g) baking potato
vegetable oil, for deep frying
sprig of flat-leaf parsley, finely chopped
Chilli Mayonnaise, to serve (page 69)
sea salt and freshly ground black pepper

★ ★ ★ ★ ★ ★ ★ ★ ★ ★ ★ ★ ★ ★ ★ ★ ★ ★ ★

Cut the chicken into 3cm pieces, then place in a large bowl. Add the garlic, onion, cheiro verde and lime juice, and season with salt and pepper. Toss to coat and leave to marinate for 20–30 minutes (or cover and chill for a couple of hours).

Put the flour, baking powder and tempero baiano seasoning in a large bowl and mix well. Peel the potato, then finely grate it over the bowl using a mandolin. The pieces should be as fine as matchsticks. Mix the potatoes with the flour until evenly coated.

Heat the oil in a deep-fat fryer to about 180°C/350°F. Add the potato and flour mixture to the bowl of marinated chicken and mix well. Fry the chicken in batches, making sure each piece is well coated with the potato matchsticks and batter. Fry each batch for 2–3 minutes, then turn it over and cook until both sides are evenly browned and crisp. Remove and drain on kitchen paper. Keep warm while frying the remaining chicken. Sprinkle with parsley and salt and serve hot, with Chilli Mayonnaise on the side.

# COXINHAS

*Coxinha* means 'little drumstick', and refers to the shape of these tasty chicken croquettes. If you asked twenty Brasilians for their recipe you'd receive a different one every time: some are made with potato, some with cheese, and some with a real chicken drumstick encased in batter. Ours are made with shredded chicken and spices, and are delicious on their own or dipped in Molho Vinagrete (page 70) or our Chilli Mayonnaise (page 69).

2 boneless, skinless chicken breasts (300–350g)
450g floury potatoes, quartered
2 tbsp olive oil
1 large onion, finely chopped
4 tbsp Spicy Malagueta Marinade (page 72)
100g plain flour
2 eggs, lightly beaten
100g panko breadcrumbs
vegetable oil, for deep-frying
few sprigs of flat-leaf parsley, finely chopped
sea salt and freshly ground black pepper

Bring a small pan of salted water to the boil, then reduce the heat to a simmer. Add the chicken and poach very gently for 10 minutes. Remove from the heat, cover and continue cooking in the residual heat for 10–15 minutes, until cooked through and firm when lightly squeezed. Remove from the liquid and leave to cool, reserving the poaching liquid.

Bring the poaching liquid to the boil and add the potatoes. Simmer for 10–15 minutes, until just tender. Drain well, then leave in the pan to dry out before mashing. Season with salt and pepper.

Meanwhile, heat the olive oil in a small pan, add the onion and cook gently, stirring, over a medium-low heat for 8–10 minutes, until soft and translucent.

To assemble, shred the chicken into small pieces and place in a large bowl. Add the mashed potatoes, onions and Spicy Malagueta Marinade. Mix well, then taste and season with salt and pepper. With damp hands, shape about 50g of the mixture into a drumstick shape, like a teardrop with a rounded base and pointed top. Set it upright on a plate and repeat with the rest of the mixture. Coat each one in flour, then egg, then breadcrumbs. Cover with clingfilm and chill for at least an hour to firm up.

Heat the oil in a deep-fryer to 170°C/325°F. Fry in batches for 3–4 minutes, turning once or twice, until golden brown. Remove and drain on kitchen paper. Serve warm, sprinkled with chopped parsley and a little more sea salt, if you like.

# PÃO DE QUEIJO

Crispy puffs of dough with a mild, cheesy flavour, *pão de queijo* are eaten for breakfast or as a snack all over Brasil. The secret to this addictive treat is the use of cassava flour *(polvilho azedo)*, which gives the balls an irresistibly moist, chewy texture. The best ones we've ever tasted were from a tiny hole-in-the-wall bakery in São Paulo, and we like to think this recipe comes pretty close.

125ml whole milk
50ml vegetable oil
1 tsp sea salt
250g cassava flour (or substitute tapioca flour)
2 eggs, lightly beaten
200g Parmesan or mature Cheddar cheese, grated

★ ★ ★ ★ ★ ★ ★ ★ ★ ★ ★ ★ ★ ★ ★ ★ ★ ★ ★ ★ ★

Put 125ml water, the milk, vegetable oil and salt in a large pan and bring to the boil. As soon as it rises up the sides of the pan, remove it from the heat. Quickly tip in the flour and stir vigorously to combine. Keep stirring until the mixture comes together as a wet dough and comes away from the side of the pan. Transfer to the bowl of a stand mixer and leave to cool slightly.

Once slightly cooled, add the eggs and start mixing at a low speed. After 1–2 minutes, increase the speed to high and beat vigorously until all the egg has been incorporated and the dough is smooth. Add the Parmesan and keep beating until the cheese is evenly mixed in.

Line a baking sheet with silicone liner or baking parchment. With damp or lightly oiled hands, roll tablespoons of the dough into small balls, about 25–30g each. You may need to wash your hands occasionally, as the dough is quite sticky. (If you have one, use a small ice-cream scoop to make this easier. Dip the scoop briefly in water, then flick away any excess water before scooping each ball.) Arrange the balls 2.5cm apart on the prepared baking sheet. You can prepare them a few hours ahead and put the tray in the fridge until you're ready to bake.

Preheat the oven to 200°C/400°F/Gas mark 6. Bake for 20–25 minutes, until puffed up and evenly golden brown. They should have a crisp exterior and a doughy, chewy centre. Serve immediately.

PÃO DE QUEIJO IN SÃO PAULO

# FOUR-CHEESE PASTELS

MAKES 24-26

Brasil has the largest Japanese community outside Japan, but because the two countries were once at war, many Japanese immigrants tried to pass as Chinese, cooking their native dishes with a Chinese accent. The *pastel* (originating from the spring roll) is one such dish, and is still enjoyed all over the country.

500g plain flour, plus extra for dusting
1½ tsp fine sea salt
1 tbsp hot chicken stock (or water)
15g lard, melted
1 tbsp cachaça
100g grated Gruyère cheese
100g cream cheese
100g feta cheese, crumbled
100g ricotta
½ tsp freshly ground black pepper
vegetable or groundnut oil, for deep-frying
Molho Vinagrete, to serve (page 70)
Mango Salsa, to serve (page 68)

★ ★ ★ ★ ★ ★ ★ ★ ★ ★ ★ ★ ★ ★ ★ ★ ★ ★ ★

First, make the dough. Put the flour and salt in a large bowl and mix well. Make a well in the centre. Stir the stock, lard, cachaça and 125ml warm water in a jug, then pour this into the well. Stir together to form a soft dough. If it's too dry and won't form a ball, gradually add more warm water until it comes together. Tip the mixture on to a lightly floured surface and knead briefly until smooth. Do not overwork it, or it will become tough. Cover with clingfilm and set aside for at least 15 minutes.

Mix together the four cheeses and black pepper in a small bowl and line a baking sheet with baking parchment. On a lightly floured surface, roll out half the dough very thinly (cover the other half in clingfilm), then cut out 10cm squares. Put 1 teaspoon filling in the centre of each square on one side. Brush a little water around the edges, then fold over the other half to make a rectangle. Press down on the edges to seal, trying not to create any air pockets. Use the tines of a fork to press down along all four sides to ensure a good seal. Continue making the rest of the pastels and transfer to the baking sheet.

Heat the oil in a deep-fryer to 180°C/350°F. Fry in batches for 3-4 minutes, until golden brown on both sides, turning them halfway. Drain on kitchen paper and keep warm while you fry the rest. Serve warm with Molho Vinagrete or Mango Salsa, if you like.

# VARIATIONS

## PRAWN & PALM HEART PASTELS

Melt 2 tablespoons butter in a pan, add a finely chopped
onion and 3 chopped garlic cloves and cook gently for
a few minutes. Skin, deseed and finely chop 2 tomatoes
and add to the pan with 1 tablespoon tomato purée. Stir
well and cook for a few minutes until the onions are
soft. Drain and roughly chop a 400g tin of palm hearts.
Roughly chop 100g cooked, peeled prawns. Add to the
pan and season well with salt and pepper. Allow to cool
before filling the pastels as described in the recipe.

## BEEF PASTELS

Heat 2 tablespoons olive oil in a wide pan, add 400g
minced beef and cook until browned. Add 1 finely
chopped spring onion, 2 chopped garlic cloves and 2
peeled, deseeded and chopped tomatoes. Fry for a few
more minutes until the tomatoes have softened. Remove
from the heat, season with salt and pepper and stir in 2
tablespoons chopped parsley. Allow to cool before filling
the pastels as described in the recipe.

# BOLINHOS

*Bolinhos* are a mainstay of Brasil's bar scene. They're little balls of rice that are lightly fried for a golden crunch, which gives way to a soft, almost creamy interior. We've incorporated the cooking of the rice into the recipe, but leftover rice can also be used. If it's quite dry, you might need to add an extra egg to help it to stick together.

150g long-grain rice
1 egg, lightly beaten
4 spring onions, trimmed and finely chopped
70g Parmesan cheese, grated, plus extra
    for sprinkling
1 tsp sea salt, or to taste
1 tsp baking powder
about 80g plain flour, plus extra for rolling
small bunch of flat-leaf parsley, finely chopped
vegetable or groundnut oil, for deep-frying
lime wedges, to serve (optional)

First, cook the rice. Put it in a pan with 400ml water and bring to the boil. Reduce the heat and simmer, part-covered, for about 10 minutes, until most of the water has been absorbed. Remove, cover and leave to steam for another few minutes. It will be slightly overcooked and sticky, and you should be able to shape it easily. Set aside to cool completely.

Add the egg, spring onions, Parmesan, salt, baking powder, half the flour and the chopped parsley (reserving 1 tablespoon) to the rice. Mix well and check the consistency: it should be stiff enough to shape into balls. If it's too sticky, gradually add more flour until you get the right consistency. With well-floured hands, roll into walnut-sized balls, about 30g each.

Heat the oil in a deep-fryer to 180°C/350°F (it should sizzle when a little rice mixture is added to it). Fry in batches for 2–3 minutes, until golden brown all over, then drain on kitchen paper. Keep warm while you fry the remaining batches. To serve, transfer to warmed bowls and serve sprinkled with grated Parmesan and the remaining parsley, and lime wedges alongside.

PÃO DE QUEIJO
COXINHAS
FOUR-CHEESE PASTELS

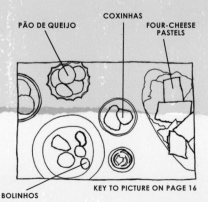

BOLINHOS
KEY TO PICTURE ON PAGE 16

# BOLINHOS DE BACALHAU

There are many variations of *bolinhos*, but the best known is the *bolinho de bacalhau*. Salt cod is a big staple of Brasilian food – it's even served as one of the main centrepiece dishes on Christmas Day.

300g salt cod
300g dry mashed potatoes (with no milk or butter)
small handful of flat-leaf parsley, finely chopped
2–3 spring onions, finely chopped
3 eggs, separated
vegetable or groundnut oil, for deep-frying
sea salt and freshly ground black pepper
lime wedges, to serve
Chilli Mayonnaise (page 69), to serve

De-salt the salt cod by soaking and rinsing it in 4–5 changes of cold water. If possible, do this over 24 hours. Drain and place it in a saucepan with enough cold water to cover. Bring to a simmer and gently poach for 5 minutes, until soft. Drain and leave to cool for a few minutes, then flake the fish and discard any skin or bones.

Put the flaked cod in a large bowl and add the mashed potatoes, parsley, spring onions and egg yolks. Mix well and season with salt and pepper. In a large, clean bowl, whisk the egg whites to stiff peaks, then fold them into the cod mixture.

Heat the oil in a deep-fryer to 180°C/350°F. If you have one, use a mini ice-cream scoop to carefully drop rough balls of cod mixture into the hot oil. Alternatively, drop in rounded teaspoons of the mixture. Fry for 1½–2½ minutes until golden brown, then turn over and cook the other side. Remove and drain on kitchen paper. Keep warm while you fry the remaining batches.

Serve warm with lime wedges and Chilli Mayonnaise.

# PULLED PORK SLIDERS

**SERVES 4 AS A MAIN COURSE**

Sliders are mini hamburgers, which are popular in the States, and here's our Brasilian take on them. The pulled pork is really worth the effort. It's even better finished on the barbecue: once cooked, add more spice mix and brown sugar, then barbecue until lightly caramelized around the edges.

**For the pulled pork**
1 tsp sea salt
1 tsp dried oregano
½ tsp caster sugar
2 tbsp ground black pepper
50g soft dark brown sugar
1 tsp cayenne pepper
1 tbsp sweet paprika
2 tbsp smoked paprika
1 tsp garlic powder
1¼ tbsp celery salt
2 tsp ground coriander
800g–1kg pork shoulder

**For the sliders**
12 freshly baked Pão de Queijo (page 13)
3½ tbsp Spicy Malagueta Marinade (page 72)
handful of flat-leaf parsley, finely chopped

Preheat the oven to 140°C/275°F/Gas mark 1. First, mix together all the ingredients except the pork in a bowl, then transfer to a clean, sealable jar. Any leftover spice mix will keep well.

Remove the rind and trim off any excess fat from the pork, then put it in a roasting pan and rub in 2–3 tablespoons of the spice mix, making sure it is evenly coated. Cover with kitchen foil and roast for 7–8 hours, until the pork is very tender and you can pull it apart with a fork. Remove and leave it to cool a little. Pull the pork into shreds with a fork or slice it thinly and moisten the meat with the juices in the pan. Any leftovers will freeze beautifully.

To assemble the sliders, slice the Pão de Queijo in half horizontally. If using leftover buns, halve and toast them before using. Mix the pork with the Spicy Malagueta Marinade and add a spoonful to each base. Top with the remaining halves and serve 3 sliders per person, sprinkled with parsley.

# CHICKEN EMPADINHAS

*Empanadas* and *empadinhas* (little ones) are savoury pies found in bars and buffet tables throughout Brasil. Traditionally, an olive is placed in the centre – the origin of the expression a *azeitona da empanada* ('an olive in the *empanada*'), which refers to something that is the crucial element. *Catupiry* is a Brasilian soft cream cheese, but it's hard to find, so you can substitute ordinary cream cheese. You can also replace the chicken with chopped canned palm hearts for a vegetarian version.

225g soft butter
450g plain flour, sifted
1¾ tsp sea salt
2 large eggs, lightly beaten
2 tbsp olive oil
1 shallot, finely chopped
2 garlic cloves, finely crushed
1 plum tomato, deseeded and finely chopped
1 tbsp tomato purée
50g peas, thawed if frozen
200g skinless and boneless cooked chicken, chopped
1 tbsp chopped flat-leaf parsley
1 tbsp chopped coriander
1 spring onion, finely chopped
pinch of ground nutmeg
100g catupiry or cream cheese
2 egg yolks mixed with 2 tbsp olive oil, to glaze
sea salt and freshly ground black pepper

First, make the pastry. Put the butter in a stand mixer and beat until pale and light. Add the flour and salt and mix at low speed until combined. Gradually add the egg, mixing until the pastry starts to come together. Try to shape an olive-sized ball of dough – if it's too dry, add 1 tablespoon cold water and mix again. Gather it into a ball, flatten it slightly, wrap it in clingfilm and chill in the fridge.

Heat the olive oil in a pan over a medium heat. Add the shallot and cook for 4–6 minutes, stirring, until soft but not browned. Add the garlic and cook for 30 seconds, until fragrant.

**CONTINUED** ⟫→

Stir in the tomato and tomato purée and cook for 2–3 minutes. Take the pan off the heat. Mix in the rest of the ingredients except the cream cheese and season with salt and pepper. Transfer to a large bowl and leave to cool before folding in the cream cheese. It should be moist and juicy, but not runny.

Preheat the oven to 180°C/350°F/Gas mark 4 and lightly butter three 12-hole mini pie or muffin tins. Roll out the dough to 3mm thick on a lightly floured surface. Use a round pastry cutter 2–3cm larger than the diameter of the holes in the tin to cut out 36 pastry circles. Press them into the prepared tins, leaving a little dough sticking out around the edge. Brush the base and sides with the egg and oil glaze. Place 1 teaspoon filling into each one. Roll out the remaining pastry and cut out 36 rounds slightly bigger than the diameter of the pies. Cover the pies with the rounds, pressing the edges together to seal. Trim off any excess dough. Brush the tops with the glaze and bake for 20–25 minutes, until golden brown. Remove and cool slightly before turning out. Serve warm.

# TOASTED GIANT CORN

This is great served with drinks as an alternative to nuts or olives. Dried giant white corn is available from South American grocers.

300g dried giant white corn (hominy)
2 tbsp vegetable oil
2 tsp sea salt
1 tsp smoked paprika

Soak the corn in a bowl of cold water for at least 12 hours or overnight. Drain and spread out to dry on a tray lined with a clean tea towel for at least 1 hour.

Heat the oil in a heavy-based frying pan over a medium heat. When the oil is hot but not smoking, add the corn kernels and toss until evenly coated with oil. Cover with a lid and cook for 10 minutes, shaking the pan occasionally, until the kernels are evenly golden and some of them have popped. If the kernels are still a bit chewy, toast them in an oven preheated to 150°C/300°F/Gas mark 2 for 10–20 minutes, stirring a few times. Remove and toss with a little salt and paprika. Leave to cool and store in an airtight container, if not serving immediately.

# SWEETCORN SOUP SHOTS

SERVES 4 AS A STARTER OR
6–8 AS SOUP SHOTS

The Portuguese colonists couldn't grow wheat in the tropical North East, so indigenous crops such as cassava and corn became a much-used substitute. Corn and cornmeal feature in many dishes from sweet desserts to savoury starters, such as this hearty soup.

20g butter
1 leek, white part only, roughly chopped
1 small onion, roughly chopped
1 celery stick, roughly chopped
200g fresh or thawed frozen sweetcorn
1 heaped tsp powdered vegetable bouillon or
    1 vegetable stock cube
sea salt and freshly ground black pepper
crème fraîche, Molho Vinagrete (page 70)
    and finely chopped flat-leaf parsley, to serve
    (optional)

Melt the butter in a heavy-based pan and add the leek, onion and celery. Cook over a medium-low heat for 8–10 minutes, stirring occasionally, until softened. Add the sweetcorn and pour in enough boiling water to cover. Stir in the vegetable bouillon powder and bring to a simmer. Cook for another 10–15 minutes, until the vegetables are very soft and tender.

Carefully transfer the soup to a blender and purée until smooth. Return the soup to the pan and season well with salt and pepper. Serve immediately or leave to cool and store in the fridge.

Reheat the soup, if necessary, and serve in warmed bowls (or espresso cups, if serving as soup shots) with a little crème fraîche, Molho Vinagrete and a sprinking of chopped parsley, if you like.

# BLACK BEAN SOUP SHOT

SERVES 4 AS A STARTER OR
6–8 AS SOUP SHOTS

This thick soup of black turtle beans, known as *caldinho de feijão* in Portuguese, is an instant shot of warmth on a cold day. We serve ours in little espresso cups topped with crème fraîche and bacon, but it's equally delicious as a starter in a large bowl or mug.

2 tbsp olive oil
1 onion, chopped
1 garlic clove, chopped
½ red chilli, deseeded and chopped
1 small carrot, chopped
1 celery stick, chopped
1 leek, trimmed and chopped
1 tbsp tomato purée
1 x 400g tin black turtle beans, drained
1 heaped tsp powdered vegetable bouillon,
  or 1 vegetable stock cube
1 sprig thyme, leaves stripped
sea salt and freshly ground black pepper
crème fraîche, crispy bacon lardons and finely
  chopped flat-leaf parsley, to serve (optional)

Heat the oil in a large pan, add the chopped vegetables and season with salt and pepper. Cook over a medium-low heat, stirring occasionally, for about 10 minutes, until softened but not coloured. Add the tomato purée and stir again. Cook for a few more minutes, then add the beans, vegetable bouillon, thyme and hot water to cover. Bring to a simmer and cook gently for 10–15 minutes, until very soft.

Carefully transfer the soup to a blender and purée until smooth. If the soup is too thick, add a splash of boiling water and blend again. Season well with salt and pepper. Serve immediately or leave to cool and store in the fridge. Reheat the soup, if necessary, and serve in warmed bowls (or espresso cups, if serving as soup shots) with a little crème fraîche, crispy bacon lardons and a sprinkling of chopped parsley, if you like.

# SWEET POTATO CRAB CAKES

**MAKES 8**

Crab cakes and fritters are wildly popular along the coast of Brasil, especially in Pelourinho, the historic centre of Salvador, Bahia. Ours have plenty of fresh crab meat, sweet potato and lime juice – a real taste of tropical Brasil.

250g or 1 large sweet potato
250g fresh white crab meat
½ green pepper, deseeded and finely chopped
½ small red onion, peeled and finely chopped
50g fresh breadcrumbs
handful of flat-leaf parsley, finely chopped
1 tbsp lime juice
1 tbsp good-quality mayonnaise
¼ tsp freshly ground black pepper
75g dried breadcrumbs
vegetable oil, for frying
sea salt and freshly ground black pepper
lime wedges, to serve
Mango Salsa (page 68), to serve

Preheat the oven to 180°C/350°F/Gas mark 4. Prick the sweet potato with a fork and wrap it in kitchen foil. Bake for 45 minutes, until soft. Remove and leave to cool slightly.

Pick through the crabmeat and remove any bits of shell. Set aside in the fridge.

Peel the potato and put the flesh in a large bowl. Mash it with a fork or potato masher. Add the pepper, onion, fresh breadcrumbs, parsley, lime juice and mayonnaise and season with salt and pepper. Mix well, then fold through the crab meat. Divide the mixture into 8, then shape each portion into a round patty and coat it with the dried breadcrumbs. Place on a tray, cover with clingfilm and chill for at least 20 minutes, until they have firmed up slightly.

When ready to cook, heat enough oil to shallow-fry the crab cakes in a large pan over a medium heat. Fry in batches for 2–4 minutes on each side, until golden brown. Remove and drain on kitchen paper. Keep warm while frying the rest. Serve warm with Mango Salsa and lime wedges on the side.

# ( KIBE )

Having been brought over by the small Lebanese community, beef and bulgur wheat balls, or *kibe*, are a wonderful illustration of Brasil's mixed culinary heritage.

150g bulgur wheat
1 tbsp vegetable or sunflower oil
1 small onion, finely chopped
3–4 garlic cloves, finely chopped
500g good-quality lean minced beef
1 tbsp finely chopped flat-leaf parsley
1 tbsp finely chopped mint
vegetable or groundnut oil, for deep-fat frying
sea salt and freshly ground black pepper
lime wedges, to serve
Chilli Mayonnaise, Mango Salsa or Molho Vinagrete
    (pages 68–70), to serve

Place the bulgur wheat in a large bowl and pour over 250ml boiling water. Cover and leave to stand for 30–45 minutes, until all the water has been absorbed.

Heat the oil in a large non-stick frying pan over a medium heat. Add the onion and half the garlic and cook for a few minutes, until softened. Season a third of the minced beef with salt and pepper and add to the pan. Break up any large chunks and cook, stirring frequently, over a high heat until the moisture has evaporated. Set aside and leave to cool.

Put the remaining beef mince in a food processor. Add the bulgur wheat, parsley, mint, remaining garlic and season with salt and pepper. Blend to a paste. Cook a little and taste it to check the seasoning, adjusting if needed. Line a large baking tray with baking parchment. Moisten your hands, take a tablespoon (about 30g) of the raw mince paste and shape it into a ball. Holding it in one hand, use the other one to make a hole in it. Fill the pocket with the cooked mince, then seal and shape it into a small rugby ball. Place on the tray and repeat with the rest of the mixture.

Heat the oil in a deep-fryer to 170°C/325°F. Fry in batches until dark brown and crisp. Remove and drain on kitchen paper, then serve warm with lime wedges and sauces to dip.

# WHEN IN RIO...

Rio de Janeiro, David's birthplace, is an ever-changing city, and never more so than in the run-up to the 2016 *Olímpicos*. Rio is known as the *cidade maravilhosa* ('wonderful city') and it has a wonderful energy. Always check for the latest (and safest) places to visit with your hotel, guide or a friendly *carioca*, as residents of Rio are called.

Here are some great experiences not to be missed!

## BEACHES

Ipanema and Leblon, separated by the canal, are the great neighbourhood beaches. There is a slightly different scene at each of the lifeguard stations (*postos*): Posto 9 is young and cool, while Posto 11 more about families from affluent Leblon. Copacabana is over-rated, in my opinion, but it remains a wonderful sweep of beach, especially at night. Surfing at Arpoador, the rocky point between Ipanema and Copacabana, is only for the experienced!

## FUTEBOL

Football is the national sport, and it's always worth going to see a match even if you are not a fan. It's a raucous occasion full of beer, snacks and music. The Maracanã stadium hosted the World Cup in 1950 and 2014 and never disappoints: the atmosphere is electric for any match. Or go and watch one of Rio's top teams – Botafogo, Flamengo, Fluminense or Vasco da Gama – to feel some of the local rivalry.

## THE GREAT OUTDOORS

Hang-glide from the top of the Tijuca Forest and land on São Conrado beach. Or walk through the extraordinary Jardim Botânico, especially on a rainy day, perhaps as far as the Cachoeira do Horto waterfall; being regaled by birds and monkeys, it's easy to forget you are in a vibrant city.

The Sugarloaf is perhaps the most famous of the many hills (*morros*) which divide Rio. Instead of taking the cable-car, you can arrange to climb up the 1,300ft mountain with a guide. Try to arrive at the top in time to see the sunset behind Christ on top of the Corcovado.

And of course, take the train to the top of the Corcovado to see Christ the Redeemer, Rio's best-known monument and a staggering achievement. Don't miss his little stone heart. It gets very busy, so go early.

## NEIGHBOURHOODS

Quite the most charming neighbourhood is the hillside district of Santa Teresa. Thankfully, the little yellow tram (*bonde*) is running again, so take it up there and wander the cobbled streets. When you've finished exploring, walk down the incredible Selaron Steps, one man's lifetime achievement, down to Lapa.

Lapa itself is the place to go to experience samba. Much more intimate than the annual *Carnaval*, there are lots of bars and clubs filled with locals, especially on Sunday nights. To experience the preparations for the *Carnaval* parade, visit a samba school (*escola de samba*): Salgueiro rehearses every Saturday in their Tijuca headquarters, from June.

It is now possible to visit one of Rio's 900 *favelas* (shanty towns), the vibrant communities which cover the hills all over the city. Make sure you take a resident as a guide, and ideally that your visit contributes to projects within the community. Rocinha is the largest, and Vidigal has extraordinary views along the beaches.

Bicycle around Rio's lagoon, currently undergoing a major clean-up to host the 2016 Olympic rowing events.

## FOOD & DRINK

You could be forgiven for thinking that *cariocas* are always eating and drinking: there is constantly someone selling something, from the beach vendors to the *botecos* (bars) and the high-end restaurants. It is definitely worth going to one of the huge rodizio *churrascarias* to experience the ballet of waiters carrying skewers of every imaginable cut of meat. *Picanha* (the cap of rump) is the national favourite.

The Brasilian cocktail is of course the caipirinha. Do try several different flavours, but beware: it is effectively a large glass of alcohol and sugar... It goes very well with any of the ubiquitous *petiscos* (bar snacks). A small glass of ice-cold draft beer (*chopp*) is never far from hand.

Start the day with a fresh juice from one of the myriad corner shops: the super-fruit açai is now well-known outside Brasil, but I also highly recommend avocado smoothie! Or the *cafézinho*, a small, sweet glass of coffee.

# CHICKEN 'ESPÍRITO SANTO'
## WITH TOMATO & PEANUT SAUCE

**SERVES 4**

Above the beaches of Rio lies the bohemian hillside village of Santa Teresa, where crumbling colonial architecture jostles for space with folksy craft shops, and the iconic yellow *bonde* tram shuffles its way up the cobbled streets. In amongst it is Espírito Santo, an Amazonian restaurant teeming with postcards of saints, indigenous headdresses and paintings by local artists. A dish of chicken skewers lightly rolled in chopped nuts was the stand-out dish on our visit, and our recipe is a tribute to this little neighbourhood restaurant. We've served it with our take on a typical Brasilian tomato and peanut sauce.

**For the chicken skewers**
60g brasil nuts
60g cashew nuts, lightly toasted
500g skinless, boneless chicken breasts or thighs
1 large egg
½ tsp sea salt
¼ tsp freshly ground black pepper
olive oil, to drizzle

**For the tomato and peanut sauce**
30g unsalted skinless peanuts
butter, for cooking
1 small onion, chopped
2 garlic cloves, chopped
¼ tsp ground coriander
2 tbsp tomato purée
2 plum tomatoes, deseeded and chopped
80ml coconut milk
½ tsp chicken bouillon or ½ stock cube
½ tsp caster sugar
sea salt and freshly ground black pepper

★ ★ ★ ★ ★ ★ ★ ★ ★ ★ ★ ★ ★ ★ ★ ★ ★ ★ ★ ★ ★

Preheat the oven to 180°C/350°F/Gas mark 4. Put the brasil nuts, cashew nuts and peanuts in separate corners of a baking tray and bake for 10–12 minutes, or until lightly toasted. Remove and leave to cool. Set the peanuts aside. Rub the brasil nuts with a kitchen towel to remove their skins, then place in a food processor along with the cashew nuts. Pulse the nuts to make coarse crumbs with a few larger chunks. Tip into a shallow bowl and set aside.

CONTINUED ⟫→

Next, make the tomato and peanut sauce. Melt the butter in a small saucepan and add the onion, garlic and ground coriander and season with salt and pepper. Cover and cook over a medium-low heat for 6–8 minutes, stirring occasionally, until soft and translucent. Add the rest of the ingredients and the toasted peanuts and give the mixture a stir. Simmer for 8–10 minutes, or until the sauce has thickened. Transfer to a food processor and blend for about 1 minute. Taste and season with salt and pepper. Return to the pan and reheat before serving.

For the chicken skewers, preheat the oven to 180°C/350°F/Gas mark 4 and lightly oil a baking sheet. Slice the chicken into 2–3cm strips. Lightly beat the egg and season with salt and pepper. Coat the chicken strips in the egg, followed by the toasted nut crumbs. Thread the coated chicken on to metal skewers and place on the baking sheet. Drizzle with a little oil and bake for 12–15 minutes, until firm and just cooked through. Divide the skewers between warmed serving plates and serve with individual bowls of tomato and peanut sauce for dipping.

# GRILLED CRAB SHELLS

In Brasil, you'll find the classic bar snack of grilled crab (*casquinha de siri*) served in scallop or crab shells – real or plastic – but you can just as easily use a ramekin. The siri crab is common in Brasil, but any fresh white crab meat can be used for our recipe.

It's best finished with a squeeze of lime to cut through the melted cheese and bring out the flavour of the crab.

Serve with a side salad and an ice-cold beer as a summery starter.

300–400g fresh white crab meat (from an 800g–1.2kg cooked brown crab)
2 slices white bread, crusts removed
2 tbsp coconut milk mixed with 1 tbsp hot water
3 tbsp olive oil, plus extra for greasing
1 shallot, finely chopped
½ yellow pepper, deseeded and finely chopped
½ green pepper, deseeded and finely chopped
1 garlic clove, finely chopped
1 red chilli, deseeded and finely chopped
1 large plum tomato, deseeded and finely chopped
60ml white wine
15g desiccated coconut (or use freshly grated, if available)
1 tsp English mustard
juice of 1 lime, plus extra wedges to serve
small handful of coriander leaves, chopped
60g dried breadcrumbs
25g grated Parmesan cheese
20g cold butter
sea salt and freshly ground black pepper

Pick through the crab meat to remove any bits of shell. Cover and refrigerate. Tear the bread into small pieces and soak in the coconut milk for 15 minutes.

Heat the oil in a large pan over a medium heat. Add the shallot, peppers, garlic, chilli and tomato and cook for 6–8 minutes, stirring occasionally, until softened. Add the wine and simmer until reduced by half. Stir in the soaked bread and desiccated coconut and cook for 1–2 minutes. Remove from the heat and stir in the crab meat, mustard, lime juice and coriander and season with salt and pepper. If it's too dry, add a little more coconut milk. Spoon into 4 lightly oiled ramekins or clean scallop shells.

Preheat the oven to 200°C/400°F/Gas mark 6. Mix the breadcrumbs and Parmesan and sprinkle them over the crab mixture. Cut the butter into very thin slices and place over the breadcrumbs. Bake for 10–12 minutes, until lightly golden brown. (If the topping isn't browning enough, put it under the grill for 2–4 minutes). Serve hot with wedges of lime.

# FIRE UP
# THE BBQ

# SPICY MALAGUETA CHICKEN

We knew from the very beginning that we wanted to create a dish using the *malagueta* chilli, a fiery Brasilian chilli similar to the Portuguese piri-piri. *Malagueta* chillies are ubiquitous in Brasil, and you'll find a bottle of them preserved in oil, vinegar or cachaça on every table top. After months of testing, we think we've got the right balance of sticky sweetness and chilli spice for the perfect marinade. The red peppers add extra sweetness and crunch. Leftover chicken can be used to spice up a salad.

500g boneless, skinless chicken thighs
5 tbsp Spicy Malagueta Marinade (page 72)
1 large red pepper
1 quantity Honey Mustard Glaze (page 77)
sea salt and freshly ground black pepper

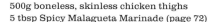

Trim off any excess fat from the chicken thighs. Place them in a bowl, add the Spicy Malagueta Marinade and toss to coat evenly. Cover with clingfilm and store in the fridge. Let the chicken marinate for at least 4 hours, preferably overnight.

Light the barbecue and let the flames die down before starting to cook. If cooking indoors, preheat the grill to medium. Deseed the pepper and cut it into 2–3cm thick strips. Thread the peppers and chicken thighs alternately on to 4 or 5 metal skewers. Season with salt and pepper and cook for 10–15 minutes, turning occasionally. Baste with the honey glaze and return to the heat for a few more minutes until golden brown and just cooked through. The chicken thighs should feel firm when ready.

Remove the skewers and leave to rest for a few minutes, then serve hot. They're great with Sweet Potato Fries (page 86).

# CAIPIRINHA 'BEER CAN' CHICKEN

SERVES 4

In Brasil, roast chicken is sometimes known as 'television chicken' (*frango de televisão*) because the family dog can often be found with its head pressed to the oven, watching it cook. Our television chicken uses the flavours of a caipirinha and a can cooking method to create a succulent, sweet and sticky roast that can be cooked on the barbecue or in the oven. The can means that the chicken steams from the inside out, making the meat extra juicy and tender.

1 medium chicken (about 1.5–1.8kg)
olive oil, for drizzling
5 sage leaves, finely chopped
2 tbsp cachaça
1 tbsp soft brown sugar
sea salt and freshly ground black pepper

**For the steam marinade**
juice of 2 large limes
2 tbsp soft brown sugar
3 tbsp cachaça
3 garlic cloves, finely chopped or crushed
½ tsp sea salt
2 tbsp olive or rapeseed oil
5–6 large sage leaves, finely chopped

★ ★ ★ ★ ★ ★ ★ ★ ★ ★ ★ ★ ★ ★ ★ ★ ★ ★ ★ ★

Light the barbecue (preferably one with a lid), and let the flames die down before starting to cook, or preheat the oven to 200°C/400°F/Gas mark 6. (If using charcoal, put most of the hot coals around the edges so there is indirect but even heat in the middle. If using a gas barbecue, set it to medium.)

Remove and discard the giblets and any excess fat in the cavity of the chicken. Rub it with a little olive oil, then rub it inside and outside with salt, pepper and chopped sage. Put all the ingredients for the steam marinade in a jug and stir to dissolve the sugar. Take an empty can and peel off any labels. Wash it out well, then pour in the marinade ingredients. Wrap the outside of a small heavy-based roasting tin with kitchen foil, then place the can in the middle. Sit the chicken on the can so that the top of it enters the cavity and the bird is upright. Spread out the legs to support the bird's weight. Take a squeezed lime half and pop it into the neck of the chicken to make a plug, or cover the neck cavity with foil to prevent the steam escaping while it cooks.

Roast for 45–55 minutes, until the chicken is almost cooked. Mix the remaining cachaça and sugar and brush it over the chicken. Cook for 10–15 minutes, until golden and the juices run clear. Remove and let rest for 10–15 minutes. Carefully transfer to a serving plate, carve and serve it drizzled with the marinade, which will have reduced to a thick and tasty sauce.

# ZINGY LIME &
# GARLIC CHICKEN

SERVES 4

As much as we love spice, we know not everyone likes a side of heat with their meal. This lime and garlic marinade results in tender, juicy chicken that's packed full of flavour, but without the chilli, therefore taking the heat down a notch.

500g skinless, boneless chicken thighs
6 tbsp Zingy Lime & Garlic Marinade (page 74)
1 yellow pepper
1 quantity Honey Mustard Glaze (page 77)
sea salt and freshly ground black pepper
lime wedges, to serve

★ ★ ★ ★ ★ ★ ★ ★ ★ ★ ★ ★ ★ ★ ★ ★ ★ ★ ★

Trim off any fat from the chicken thighs, then put them in a bowl. Add the marinade and toss to coat. Let the chicken marinate for at least 4 hours, or overnight.

Light the barbecue and let the flames die down before starting to cook. If cooking indoors, preheat the grill to high. Trim and remove the seeds from the yellow pepper and cut it into wedges. Thread alternating pepper strips and chicken thighs on to 4 or 5 metal skewers and season lightly with salt and pepper. Cook for 10–12 minutes, turning once or twice, until the chicken is almost cooked through.

Baste liberally with the honey mustard glaze, then return to the heat for another 2–3 minutes, until evenly golden brown. The chicken thighs should feel firm when ready.

Remove the skewers and leave to rest for a few minutes. Serve hot with lime wedges on the side. It's delicious with Biro-Biro Rice (page 80) and Sweet Potato Fries (page 86).

# BRASILIAN BARBECUE PARTY

Celebrate summer – and the
Olympics in Rio – with this
vibrant, simple and tasty
plan-ahead barbecue menu.
To serve 8–10 people, you'll need
to double the quantities of the
main course dishes you think
will be the most popular, and
also double up on the sauces,
greens, rice, grilled pineapple
and Coco Cabana.

## MENU

### SPICY MALAGUETA CHICKEN
(PAGE 38)

### CHIMICHURRI MONKFISH
(PAGE 60)

### CHILLI & CUMIN MARINATED HANGER STEAK
(PAGE 56)

### GRILLED PORTOBELLO MUSHROOMS WITH HALLOUMI
(PAGE 55)

### MOLHO VINAGRETE
(PAGE 70)

### CORNBREAD
(PAGE 84)

### BIRO-BIRO RICE
(PAGE 80)

### STIR-FRIED GREENS WITH GARLIC
(PAGE 82)

### GRILLED PINEAPPLE
(PAGE 64)

### COCONUT & LIME SORBET
(PAGE 94)

### COCO CABANA
(PAGE 122)

## THE DAY BEFORE

+ Make the Spicy Malagueta Marinade, put it on the chicken and marinate in the fridge overnight.

✕ Make and freeze the Coconut & Lime Sorbet (one quantity will give one small scoop per person, which is fine as an accompaniment to the grilled pineapple, but double the quantities if you want to have plenty).

## FOUR HOURS BEFORE GUESTS ARRIVE

+ Make the Chimichurri Marinade, put it on the monkfish and refrigerate.

✕ Cut the large pineapple into rings and refrigerate. Prepare the glaze.

✕ Make the Molho Vinagrete.

+ Prepare the portobello mushrooms for grilling.

✕ Prepare and bake the cornbread.

## ONE HOUR BEFORE GUESTS ARRIVE

+ Make the Biro-Biro Rice.

✕ Thread the Spicy Malagueta Chicken onto the skewers.

## TWENTY MINUTES BEFORE GUESTS ARRIVE

✕ Light the barbecue (see page 48).

+ Grill the pineapple on the barbecue while the grates are still clean, then set aside.

✕ Make a large jug of Coco Cabana and chill it (but don't add the ice just yet).

## WHEN GUESTS ARRIVE

+ Add the ice to the Coco Cabana and serve.

✕ Grill the Portobello Mushrooms and Chimichurri Monkfish.

✕ Make the Stir-Fried Greens with Garlic and slice the cornbread.

+ Grill the Spicy Malagueta Chicken and Pork in a Parmesan Crust.

✕ Serve the grilled meats and fish with the sides and Molho Vinagrete.

✕ When ready for dessert, serve the Grilled Pineapple with Coconut & Lime Sorbet.

# CACHAÇA
# GRILLED CHICKEN

**SERVES 4**

On a trip to Rio, David's old friend Miguel took us to his favourite *galetaria* (chicken shop), Sat's Galeto, and introduced us to a dish we instantly knew we wanted to include: chicken breast, flattened and butterflied, marinated in cachaça and oregano and lightly grilled. It's an original and crowd-pleasing addition to the barbecue.

500g boneless, skinless chicken thighs
3 garlic cloves, finely crushed
½ tsp dried or fresh chopped oregano
4 tbsp cachaça
2 tbsp olive oil
1 tsp sea salt
½ tsp freshly ground black pepper
few sprigs flat-leaf parsley, finely chopped
lime wedges, to serve (optional)

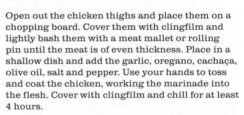

Open out the chicken thighs and place them on a chopping board. Cover them with clingfilm and lightly bash them with a meat mallet or rolling pin until the meat is of even thickness. Place in a shallow dish and add the garlic, oregano, cachaça, olive oil, salt and pepper. Use your hands to toss and coat the chicken, working the marinade into the flesh. Cover with clingfilm and chill for at least 4 hours.

Remove the chicken from the fridge half an hour before you start cooking and let it come to room temperature. Light the barbecue and let the flames die down before starting to cook. If cooking indoors, heat a griddle pan until hot. If you like, thread the chicken on to metal skewers, which will make it easier to turn them on the barbecue. Cook on the griddle or barbecue for 3–5 minutes on each side, until just cooked through – the chicken should feel firm when lightly pressed. Leave to rest for 5 minutes before serving with a sprinkling of chopped parsley and lime wedges on the side. We like to serve it with Grilled Portobello Mushrooms with Halloumi (page 55) and Bahian-Spiced Aubergine (page 62).

# CABANA'S BARBECUING DO'S & DON'TS

## DO

♥ Soak wooden skewers in cold water for at least 30 minutes before you use them, to prevent them scorching. If using metal skewers, wipe them with a piece of kitchen towel dipped in vegetable oil to stop food from sticking to them.

♥ Place bundles of fresh, hard-stemmed herbs and whole garlic cloves on the coals to add flavour to your food. Aromatic wood chips also work well.

♥ Make sure meat is cooked properly: check it is piping hot all the way through and that chicken or pork juices are running clear.

Leave time to get the meat up to room temperature before placing it on the grill. This will ensure that it cooks at an even rate.

♥ Be patient with charcoal. It takes 30 minutes to reach cooking temperature and should be white when you start to cook on it.

## DON'T

✗ Leave meat in the middle of the barbecue for the entire cooking time. Place foods near the hot coals to sear the exterior at the beginning, then move further away to prevent the outside from burning before the inside is cooked.

✗ Leave all the preparation for your side dishes until you've started barbecuing, or you'll be faced with a mad rush.

✗ Poke the meat with anything sharp while it cooks, or the juices will escape; invest in a pair of tongs and put the meat on a side plate to check it.

✗ Let individual pieces of food touch on the grill. Keeping the meat separated will help it cook on all sides.

And finally,

✗ Be frustrated if the weather lets you down. Just heat up your grill oven, mix yourself a caipirinha and say <u>tudo bem</u>: everything's good.

# PICANHA BURGER

SERVES 4

This Anglo-Brasilian dish combines Brasil's favourite cut of meat with Britain's favourite barbecue dish. If you can't find *picanha* (cap of rump), or would prefer something lighter, you can substitute the same amount of good-quality minced beef. Potato matchsticks, or 'chipsticks', are popular in Brasil. You can find matchstick potatoes in larger supermarkets (they're sometimes called potato sticks or straw potatoes) or in specialist Latin American stores.

500g picanha, hand minced (or ask the butcher to mince it for you)
30g dried breadcrumbs
3-4 tbsp Chilli & Cumin Marinade (page 76)
olive oil, for brushing
4 brioche burger buns
4-5 tbsp Black Beans (page 81)
4 tsp Chilli Mayonnaise (page 69)
3 plum tomatoes, sliced
4 tsp Chimichurri Marinade (page 73)
handful of matchstick potatoes (optional)
sea salt and freshly ground black pepper

★ ★ ★ ★ ★ ★ ★ ★ ★ ★ ★ ★ ★ ★ ★ ★ ★ ★ ★

First, make the burgers. Put the beef mince and breadcrumbs in a large bowl, add the Chilli & Cumin Marinade, season with salt and pepper and mix well. Fry a teaspoon to taste it and check the seasoning; adjust if necessary. Divide the mince into 4 portions and moisten your hands. Shape each portion into a flat burger patty. Cover and chill the patties for at least 30 minutes to firm up.

Light the barbecue and let the flames die down before starting to cook. If cooking indoors, heat a griddle pan until very hot. If using a griddle pan, reduce the heat to medium, then lightly oil the patties and cook for 4-6 minutes on each side, until cooked to medium well. If using the barbecue, you may need to move them to a cooler section once browned. Remove and leave to rest for a few minutes.

Meanwhile, slice and toast the burger buns and warm up the black beans in a pan. To assemble, put the bottom halves of the buns on 4 serving plates, then spread the top halves with Chilli Mayonnaise. Arrange 3 tomato slices on each bun base and place a burger on top. Spoon over a little Chimichurri Marinade, followed by a tablespoon of black beans. Sprinkle the beans with potato matchsticks, if using, then add the burger bun tops. Serve immediately.

# CHILLI & CUMIN MARINATED LAMB

SERVES 4

Beef is generally preferred over lamb in Brasil, but Chilli & Cumin Lamb has been one of the most popular dishes we've served at Cabana. We use lamb fillet because we think it's the most tender cut, but you could use diced leg or rump if you prefer. The palm hearts bring out the earthiness of the lamb.

600g lamb fillet
6 tbsp Chilli & Cumin Marinade (page 76)
400g tinned palm hearts, drained
sea salt and freshly ground black pepper

★ ★ ★ ★ ★ ★ ★ ★ ★ ★ ★ ★ ★ ★ ★ ★ ★ ★ ★ ★ ★

Trim off any tough outer membranes from the lamb, then cut each fillet into evenly sized cubes, about 4cm each. Place in a bowl and toss with 4 tablespoons of the Chilli & Cumin Marinade. Cover with clingfilm and leave to marinate in the fridge for at least 4 hours, or preferably overnight.

Light the barbecue and let the flames die down before starting to cook. If cooking indoors, preheat the grill to medium and place the grill rack at the highest level. Cut each palm heart in half, then thread them on to metal skewers, alternating with the marinated lamb pieces. Season lightly with salt and pepper, then cook for 8–10 minutes, turning the skewers a few times, until evenly browned. The lamb is best cooked medium rare, and it should feel slightly springy when pressed.

Remove the skewers and brush with the remaining marinade. Rest for 5–10 minutes before serving. It works well with sides such as Black Beans (page 81).

# GRILLED SEA BASS IN BANANA LEAVES

SERVES 4

Wrapping fish in banana leaves is popular in Brasil, where banana trees grow in abundance. Banana leaves are available in Asian or Latin American grocers, but you can substitute kitchen foil. You could also use other firm white fish such as sea bream, hake or whiting.

4 small whole sea bass (about 500–550g each), scaled and gutted
4 large banana leaves
4 limes, sliced
8 thick slices fresh root ginger
2 garlic cloves, thinly sliced
2 red chillies (preferably malagueta chillies), thinly sliced
large handful of mint leaves, roughly chopped

**For the marinade**
4 tbsp olive oil, plus extra for brushing
finely grated zest and juice of 1 lime
2 tsp soft brown sugar
sea salt and freshly ground black pepper

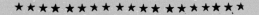

Light the barbecue, preferably one with a lid, and let the flames die down before starting to cook. Alternatively, preheat the oven to 200°C/400°F/Gas mark 6. Soak 8 wooden cocktail sticks for at least 20 minutes.

Rinse the sea bass and pat it dry with kitchen paper, then score the flesh on both sides. In a small bowl, combine all the ingredients for the marinade. Open the banana leaves and brush each one with a little olive oil. Place a sea bass in the middle of each leaf, then spoon over the marinade. Stuff the belly cavities of the fish with the sliced lime, ginger, garlic, chillies and mint leaves. Wrap the banana leaf around each one to form a loose parcel, then secure the ends with the cocktail sticks.

Place the parcels on the barbecue and close the lid, if you have one. Alternatively, cook on a baking tray in the oven. Cook for 20–25 minutes, depending on the size and thickness of the parcels of the fish. Serve in the parcels. It's great with Grilled Pineapple (page 64), Mango Salsa (page 68) and rice.

# GRILLED PORTOBELLO MUSHROOMS
# WITH HALLOUMI

SERVES 4

On the beaches of Brasil you'll often come across men selling *queijo coalho*, a firm white cheese, grilled on skewers and often sprinkled with oregano and drizzled with molasses.
Halloumi has the same squeaky texture and ability to withstand the heat of the barbecue. The cheese's saltiness works beautifully with the soft juiciness of the mushrooms.

8 large or 12 small Portobello mushrooms
3 garlic cloves, finely crushed
few sprigs thyme, leaves stripped
4 tbsp olive oil, plus extra to drizzle
250g halloumi cheese, sliced
small handful of flat-leaf parsley, finely chopped
sea salt and freshly ground black pepper

Light the barbecue, preferably one with a lid, and let the flames die down before starting to cook. If cooking indoors, preheat the grill to medium. Brush any dirt off the mushrooms and trim the stalks. Lightly oil a baking sheet and arrange the mushrooms on top, bottom-side up. Mix the garlic, thyme and oil in a small bowl, season with salt and pepper and spoon it over the mushrooms. Drizzle the edges with a little olive oil, then season with black pepper.

Cook the mushrooms over indirect heat on the barbecue or place the baking sheet under the hot grill for 7–8 minutes. When the mushrooms are cooked and tender, carefully place the halloumi slices on top. Return to the heat and cook for a couple more minutes, until the cheese has softened and is lightly golden around the edges. (If using the barbecue, you may need to cover it with a lid in order for the halloumi to melt and colour slightly.) Sprinkle with parsley and serve immediately, as the cheese will toughen as it cools.

# CHILLI & CUMIN MARINATED HANGER STEAK

SERVES 4

At traditional Brasilian *churrascarias*, rock salt is usually sprinkled on the side of meat that faces the grill, then knocked off just before serving. It's tasty just like that, but we've adapted our steak to include a bit more spice. Our Chilli & Cumin Marinade is a blend of vinegar, cumin seeds, oregano and chilli flakes; we use it to marinate all our steaks, but it's equally good on lamb or fish.

4 x 200g hanger steaks (also known as butcher's steak or onglet)
4 tbsp Chilli & Cumin Marinade (page 76), plus extra for brushing
olive oil, for brushing
sea salt and freshly ground black pepper

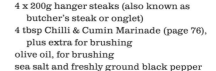

Put the steaks in a large bowl and toss with the marinade. Cover with clingfilm and chill for at least 4 hours, or preferably overnight.

Half an hour before you are ready to cook, take the steaks out of the fridge and let them come to room temperature. Light the barbecue and let the flames die down before starting to cook. If cooking indoors, heat a griddle pan until very hot. Scrape the marinade off the steaks and pat dry with kitchen paper. Brush them with a little oil, season lightly with salt and pepper, then barbecue or griddle for 3–4 minutes on each side, or until cooked to medium rare. They should feel a little springy when pressed. Remove from the heat and brush with a little marinade. Leave to rest for 5–10 minutes before serving. We like our steaks with Sweet Potato Fries (page 86) and a salad.

# MALAGUETA JUMBO PRAWNS

SERVES 4

Prawns and barbecues are a match made in heaven: the tasty crustaceans are easy to grill, taste great with a slight char, and make an interesting alternative to the usual bacon and bangers. Try them with our Spicy Malagueta Marinade for an added kick.

12 large tiger prawns or 20 ordinary prawns
4 tbsp Spicy Malagueta Marinade (page 72)
sea salt and freshly ground black pepper
lime wedges, to serve

★ ★ ★ ★ ★ ★ ★ ★ ★ ★ ★ ★ ★ ★ ★ ★ ★ ★ ★

Peel and devein the prawns, but leave the tail ends on. Place them in a bowl and add 3 tablespoons Spicy Malagueta Marinade. Toss to coat, cover with clingfilm and leave to marinate in the fridge for a couple of hours.

Light the barbecue and let the flames die down before starting to cook. If cooking indoors, preheat the grill to high and place the grill rack at the highest level. Thread the prawns on to 4 metal skewers, then brush with the remaining marinade and season with salt and pepper. Barbecue or grill for about 2–3 minutes on each side, until they have turned opaque and are just cooked through. Serve with lime wedges on the side. They're delicious with Biro-Biro Rice (page 80) and a side salad.

# CHIMICHURRI MONKFISH

SERVES 4

Cooking fish on a barbecue can be tricky because it can easily flake and fall apart, but monkfish is firm enough to withstand the heat. You can use monkfish cheeks as we've done here, which are succulent and delicious, or ask your fishmonger for monkfish tails to grill whole and slice. The herby chimichurri marinade works brilliantly with it.

12 monkfish cheeks, about 500g in total
    (or use monkfish tails)
4 tbsp Chimichurri Marinade (page 73)
sea salt and freshly ground black pepper

★ ★ ★ ★ ★ ★ ★ ★ ★ ★ ★ ★ ★ ★ ★ ★ ★ ★ ★

Trim off any tough outer membrane from the monkfish, then put it in a bowl and toss with the marinade until evenly coated. Cover with clingfilm and chill for at least 4 hours.

Light the barbecue and let the flames die down before starting to cook. If cooking indoors, preheat the grill to high and place the grill rack at the highest level. Alternatively, you could also pan-fry the fish over a medium heat. Thread the monkfish on to 4 metal skewers and season lightly with salt and pepper. Barbecue or grill the skewers for 2–3 minutes on each side. The fish should be opaque and feel just firm when lightly pressed. Allow to rest for about 5 minutes before serving.

We like to serve the dish with Biro-Biro Rice (page 80) and Toasted Farofa (page 68).

# BAHIAN-SPICED
# AUBERGINE

SERVES 4–6 AS A SIDE DISH OR 2 AS A MAIN COURSE

*Tempero baiano* is a spice mixture from Bahia in eastern Brasil, which is often used to flavour fish, vegetables and soups. This is far more exciting than the usual vegetarian barbecue options, and can also be served as a side dish with barbecued meat.

1 large or 2 medium aubergines
olive oil, for brushing
2–3 tsp Chimichurri Marinade (page 73)
2–3 tsp Spicy Malagueta Marinade (page 72)
sea salt and freshly ground black pepper

**For the tempero baiano seasoning**
1 tsp cumin seeds
½ tsp dried parsley
½ tsp ground turmeric
½ tsp ground white peppercorns
¼ tsp cayenne pepper
1 tsp dried oregano

★ ★ ★ ★ ★ ★ ★ ★ ★ ★ ★ ★ ★ ★ ★ ★ ★ ★ ★

Light the barbecue and let the flames die down before starting to cook. If cooking indoors, heat a griddle pan until hot. Mix together all the spices for the seasoning and set aside. Cut the aubergine into 1.5cm thick slices. Brush the slices with olive oil, then sprinkle over the spice mixture and season lightly with salt and pepper. Thread the slices on to metal skewers.

Barbecue or griddle the aubergine slices for 2–4 minutes on each side, until tender and golden brown around the edges. Transfer to a serving plate, drizzle over a little of the Chimichurri and Spicy Malagueta marinades and serve warm.

# GRILLED PINEAPPLE

SERVES 6–8

This dish can be sweet or savoury – it's up to you. The sweetness of the pineapple works well as a side dish with grilled meat or fish, or you can serve it with a scoop of ice cream or dollop of crème fraîche for an easy dessert.

1 medium pineapple
3 tbsp runny honey
juice of ½ lime
pinch of sea salt

★ ★ ★ ★ ★ ★ ★ ★ ★ ★ ★ ★ ★ ★ ★ ★ ★ ★ ★ ★

Cut the top and bottom off the pineapple, then stand it upright on a chopping board and slice off the skin all the way around. Remove any remaining eyes (the brown dots) with a small sharp knife. Turn the pineapple on its side and slice it into 1cm thick rounds. Use a small round pastry cutter to stamp out and discard the hard central core from each slice.

Light the barbecue and let the flames die down before starting to cook. If cooking indoors, lightly oil a griddle pan and heat until medium hot. In a small bowl, combine the honey, lime juice and salt to make a glaze. Brush the glaze over the pineapple slices, then barbecue or griddle them for 2–3 minutes on each side, or until caramelized around the edges. Turn the pineapple as it cooks, brushing it with a little more of the glaze. Drizzle the grilled pineapple with any leftover glaze and serve immediately.

# A LITTLE SOMETHING ON THE SIDE

# TOASTED FAROFA

SERVES 4–6 AS AN ACCOMPANIMENT

Farofa is a flour made from ground cassava root. Toasted, it can be used to stuff chicken or fish, but is most often used as a side dish for grilled meats or stews to give them a savoury crunch. Meat eaters can fry 125g chopped smoky bacon until golden brown before adding the farofa. Cassava meal, known as *farinha de mandioca*, is available from specialist Latin American shops or online.

50g butter or olive oil
1 small red onion, finely chopped
1 garlic clove, finely chopped
200g cassava (manioc) meal

★ ★ ★ ★ ★ ★ ★ ★ ★ ★ ★ ★ ★ ★ ★ ★ ★ ★

Melt the butter or oil in a frying pan over a medium heat. Add the onion and cook for 6–8 minutes, stirring frequently, until soft. Stir in the garlic and cook for 1 more minute, then add the cassava meal. Cook, stirring frequently, for 5–10 minutes, until it is lightly golden brown and resembles toasted breadcrumbs. It's best eaten immediately, but any leftovers can be reheated in a frying pan.

 # MANGO SALSA

SERVES 4

Mangoes grow in abundance in Brasil's tropical climate, in a rainbow of varieties. Juicy with mango flesh, tart and piquant with lime juice and chilli, this mango salsa is excellent with seafood, such as the Sweet Potato Crab Cakes (page 28), and also pairs nicely with grilled chicken and pork.

1 small ripe mango
1 red onion, finely chopped
2 spring onions, finely chopped
1 red or green chilli, deseeded and
    finely chopped
juice and zest of ½ lime
few sprigs of coriander, leaves chopped
sea salt and freshly ground black pepper

Peel the mango and cut off the flesh around the seed. Slice the flesh into 1cm dice and place in a large bowl. Add the rest of the ingredients, stir well and season with salt and pepper. Serve soon after preparing, as the coriander will darken once exposed to the lime juice.

# CHILLI MAYONNAISE

**MAKES ABOUT 350ML**

Slather this on our Picanha Burger (page 49), use it as a dip for Sweet Potato Fries (page 86), or serve it alongside street food snacks.

2 large egg yolks
1 tsp English mustard
1¼ tsp Dijon mustard
240ml rapeseed or vegetable oil
80ml light olive oil
1 tsp white wine vinegar (optional)
1¼ tsp lemon juice
½ tsp sea salt
2 tbsp tomato purée
1½ tbsp sweet chilli sauce, or to taste

Put the egg yolks and mustards in a small food processor and blend for a few minutes, until thick. Meanwhile, mix the rapeseed and olive oils together in a jug. With the motor running, slowly add the oil to the egg mixture in brief trickles, ensuring the mixture emulsifies. If it gets too stiff, add the vinegar to thin it down. If it curdles, pour it into a clean bowl, then add an egg yolk to the food processor and gradually whisk in the curdled mixture, followed by the rest of the oil.

Once about a third of the oil has been added, start drizzling in the rest in a steady stream, still blending. When all the oil has been incorporated, season with the lemon juice and salt. Finally, blend in the tomato purée and sweet chilli sauce. Keep refrigerated until ready to serve. It is best eaten within a week.

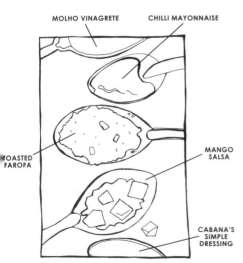

MOLHO VINAGRETE     CHILLI MAYONNAISE

TOASTED
FAROFA

MANGO
SALSA

CABANA'S
SIMPLE
DRESSING

KEY TO PICTURE ON PAGE 71

# CABANA'S SIMPLE DRESSING

**MAKES ABOUT 700ML**

This is easy to make, and perfect for pepping up fresh green leaves.

3¼ tbsp Dijon mustard
4 tbsp tarragon vinegar
625ml extra-virgin olive oil
1 garlic clove, finely crushed
squeeze of lemon juice
½ tsp caster sugar, or to taste
¼ tsp sea salt, or to taste

Put the mustard and vinegar in a bowl and whisk well. Slowly whisk in the oil, ensuring the mixture emulsifies. Whisk in the rest of the ingredients and season with salt and pepper. Pour into a clean bottle or jar, seal and keep refrigerated. Use within a week or two.

 # MOLHO VINAGRETE

**SERVES 4**

*Molho* literally means 'sauce' in Portuguese, and *molho vinagrete* is a typical sauce used at Brasilian barbecues. The tangy flavours work well with most barbecue dishes.

3 ripe plum tomatoes (about 250g)
1 small onion
small handful of flat-leaf parsley
1 tbsp white wine vinegar
3 tbsp light olive oil
sea salt and freshly ground black pepper

Halve the tomatoes, scoop out the seeds with a teaspoon, chop them and place in a large bowl. Chop the onion to about the same size as the tomatoes and add to the bowl. Finely chop the parsley leaves and add them to the bowl.

Whisk the vinegar, oil and a pinch each of salt and pepper to make a dressing. Drizzle it over the tomato mixture and stir well. Spoon into one large or small individual bowls to serve.

# SPICY MALAGUETA MARINADE

MAKES ABOUT 275ML

This is Cabana's signature marinade and is used in our Spicy Malagueta Chicken and Jumbo Prawns (pages 38 and 58). The seeds are usually left in the chillies for heat, but you could remove them if you prefer a milder flavour.

70g small red chillies
  (preferably malagueta)
5 garlic cloves, lightly crushed
70ml light olive or sunflower oil
2 tbsp lemon juice
2½ tsp tomato purée
2½ tsp caster sugar
½ tsp dried chilli flakes
1 heaped tbsp sweet paprika
2 tsp sea salt
pinch of dried oregano

Preheat the oven to 180°C/350°F/Gas mark 4. Split the chillies lengthways and place them in a small roasting tray with the garlic and olive oil. Roast for 10 minutes. Leave to cool for a few minutes, then put the chillies, garlic and oil in a small food processor or blender and add the rest of the ingredients. Blend to a smooth purée. Transfer to a clean jar, seal and keep refrigerated for up to a week.

# CHIMICHURRI MARINADE

**MAKES ABOUT 175ML**

Chimichurri is a fresh herb marinade that's Argentinian in origin, but has been adopted by Brasilian *churrascarias* (barbecue restaurants) as a marinade for steak and fish. It also works well with vegetables. We use it with Chimichurri Monkfish (page 60) and Grilled Portobello Mushrooms with Halloumi (page 55); you can also serve it as a dipping sauce with slices of fresh sourdough bread.

30g flat-leaf parsley
5 large garlic cloves
1 tsp dried oregano
150ml light olive or sunflower oil
½ tsp dried chilli flakes
35ml red wine vinegar
1 tsp sea salt
1 tsp freshly ground black pepper

★ ★ ★ ★ ★ ★ ★ ★ ★ ★ ★ ★ ★ ★ ★ ★ ★ ★

Bring a small pan of water to the boil and have a bowl of iced water ready. Blanch the parsley for 1 minute, then drain it immediately and plunge it into the icy water. Drain and pat dry with kitchen paper.

Finely chop the parsley and garlic and place it in a bowl or a clean jar with lid. Add the rest of the ingredients and stir well. Alternatively, blend the blanched parsley with the rest of the ingredients in a food processor. Use immediately, or refrigerate in a sealed container and use within 3–4 days.

# ZINGY LIME
# & GARLIC MARINADE

This is a milder marinade we use for chicken. It's a good alternative for anyone who's not partial to chillies.

1 large onion, roughly chopped
5 large garlic cloves, roughly chopped
100ml lime juice
4 tbsp rapeseed or vegetable oil
4 tbsp mirin (Japanese sweetened rice wine)
40g flat-leaf parsley, roughly chopped
40g coriander, roughly chopped
1 tsp sea salt
1 tsp freshly ground black pepper

★ ★ ★ ★ ★ ★ ★ ★ ★ ★ ★ ★ ★ ★ ★ ★ ★ ★ ★ ★

Put all the ingredients in a small food processor or blender and process until the herbs and garlic are finely chopped and you end up with a loose, wet paste. Use immediately or keep refrigerated in a clean sealed jar. It will keep well for a few days, although it may lose its vibrant green colour over time.

# CHILLI & CUMIN MARINADE

This is a warming and subtly spiced marinade that we use for our Chilli & Cumin Marinated Hanger Steak (page 56) and Picanha Burger (page 49).

70g red chillies (preferably malagueta), deseeded and roughly chopped
5–6 garlic cloves, roughly chopped
3 tbsp mirin (Japanese sweetened rice wine)
2 tbsp red wine vinegar
2 tsp sea salt
1 heaped tsp toasted cumin seeds
½ tsp dried oregano
60ml light olive or sunflower oil

Put all the ingredients in a small food processor and blend to a smooth, wet paste suitable for coating meats and fish. Use immediately or refrigerate for up to a week in a clean sealed jar.

# HONEY MUSTARD GLAZE

**MAKES ABOUT 50ML**

This sticky glaze adds a great finishing touch to grilled meat and chicken.

2 tbsp honey
1 tbsp cider vinegar
1 tsp Dijon mustard

Stir all the ingredients together in a small bowl and use to brush over grilled meat to glaze it.

CHILLI & CUMIN MARINADE

CHIMICHURRI MARINADE

CHILLI MAYONNAISE

ZINGY LIME & GARLIC MARINADE

KEY TO PICTURE ON FOLLOWING PAGE

SPICY MALAGUETA MARINADE

# BIRO-BIRO RICE

SERVES 4

Antônio José da Silva Filho, better known as Biro-Biro, is a retired Brasilian footballer. It seems he loved this dish of stir-fried rice topped with crispy onions so much that the Brasilians named it after him. It can be served alongside most dishes, like Spicy Malagueta Chicken (page 38). Any leftovers can be used to make crunchy rice Bolinhos (page 18).

**For the crispy shallots**
vegetable or groundnut oil, for deep-frying
¾ tsp sea salt
75g plain flour
1 banana shallot, sliced into thin half-moons
100ml milk

**For the rice**
200g basmati rice
3 tbsp olive oil
1 red onion, finely chopped
4 spring onions, chopped
small handful of flat-leaf parsley, chopped
sea salt and freshly ground black pepper

First, make the crispy shallots. Heat the oil in a deep-fat fryer to 190°C/375°F. Mix the salt with the flour and coat the shallot slices with it: put it all in a small plastic bag, hold tightly and shake well, then tip out into a sieve and shake off any excess. Dip the coated slices in milk, drain, then coat again with the flour. Shake off any excess. Fry in batches until golden brown, then remove and drain on kitchen paper. Sprinkle with salt while hot.

Wash the rice in cold running water. Drain, put in a small saucepan with 350ml water and bring to the boil. Reduce the heat to a simmer, cover and cook for 10 minutes, until it has absorbed most of the water. Remove from the heat and leave to steam, covered, for 10 minutes.

Heat the oil in a large pan, add the red onions and season with salt. Fry over a medium heat for 6–8 minutes, until softened. Add the rice and stir well. Stir in the spring onions and parsley. Season with salt and pepper. Serve warm, topped with the crispy shallots.

# BLACK BEANS

SERVES 4

Brasilians love black beans *(feijão)* so much that apparently, during World War II when fuel was rationed, savvy housewives would dig an outdoor cooking pit to cook them very slowly, using as little fuel as possible. The traditional recipe uses dried beans, which involves soaking them overnight and using a pressure cooker, but use tinned beans to save time. You could add bacon lardons to the pot if you'd like a meatier flavour.

2 tbsp olive oil
1 large onion, finely chopped
1 garlic clove, finely chopped
1 small carrot, finely diced
1 celery stick, finely diced
½ tsp ground cumin
½ tsp paprika
1½ tbsp tomato purée
2 x 400g tins black beans in water
1 heaped tsp vegetable bouillon powder
  (or 1 vegetable stock cube)
few sprigs of thyme, leaves stripped
200g lardons (optional)
sea salt and freshly ground black pepper

★ ★ ★ ★ ★ ★ ★ ★ ★ ★ ★ ★ ★ ★ ★ ★ ★ ★ ★

Heat the oil in a large saucepan, add the chopped vegetables and cook over a medium-low heat, stirring occasionally, for 8–10 minutes, until softened. Stir in the spices and cook for a further 2–3 minutes until they release their fragrance. Add the tomato purée, the black beans and their liquid, the vegetable bouillon and thyme and give it a good stir. Simmer for 10–12 minutes to reduce some of the liquid.

If using lardons, heat a little olive oil in a large saucepan over a medium heat, add the lardons and cook for 5–10 minutes until the fat has rendered out and they are crispy and brown. Add to the beans just before serving.

Taste and season with salt and pepper. Serve in warmed bowls.

# STIR-FRIED GREENS WITH GARLIC

**SERVES 4**

There's an old wives' tale in Brasil that a woman was only ready for marriage if she knew how to kill, pluck and cook a chicken and finely slice a bunch of collard greens. Stir-fried collard greens, or *couve* ('ku-veh') as they are called in Brasil, is a dish from the Minas Gerais region and is a popular accompaniment to feijoada or as part of the *prato executivo* (businessman's lunch).

400g seasonal greens (such as mustard greens, Swiss chard, sweetheart cabbage, spinach or young kale)
2 tbsp olive oil
3 large garlic cloves, finely chopped
butter, for cooking
sea salt and freshly ground black pepper

★ ★ ★ ★ ★ ★ ★ ★ ★ ★ ★ ★ ★ ★ ★ ★ ★ ★ ★

Wash the greens well, then remove any tough stalks and chop or shred the leaves (extra finely, if your future mother-in-law is watching).

Heat the oil in a large pan or wok over a medium heat. Add the garlic and let it gently infuse with the oil for a few minutes, without allowing it to burn. When you begin to smell the aroma of the garlic, and before it begins to colour, add the greens a handful at a time, stirring well each time. Season with salt and pepper and add a tiny splash of water. Stir well and cover with a lid. Cook until just tender (cooking time will vary from 2–10 minutes, depending on the type of greens, so taste a little every few minutes to check). Stir in the butter and check the seasoning. Transfer to warmed bowls and serve immediately.

# CORNBREAD

SERVES 8

Cornbread, or *broa de milho*, is a traditional Portuguese dish that's baked in a wood-fired oven and eaten at festivals. There's also a sweet version, *bolo de milho*, which is often studded with guava paste. Savoury cornbread is usually served with soups for dunking, or with *linguiça* sausage, but we think it also goes well with grilled dishes, American barbecue style.

100g fine cornmeal or polenta
100g plain flour
¾ tsp sea salt
1 tbsp baking powder
½ tsp baking soda
75g caster sugar
2 large eggs
150ml buttermilk
4 tbsp olive oil, plus extra for greasing
200g creamed sweetcorn

Preheat the oven to 180°C/350°F/Gas mark 4. Lightly grease a 20cm square baking tin with olive oil and line the base with baking parchment.

Sift all the dry ingredients into a large bowl. Beat the eggs, buttermilk and oil together in a separate bowl. Pour the egg mixture into the dry ingredients and fold it through. Finally, fold in the creamed sweetcorn, then pour into the prepared tin and spread out evenly.

Bake for 20–25 minutes, until it is golden brown and a skewer inserted in the middle of the cornbread comes out clean. Remove and leave to cool slightly. Cut into 16 squares and serve warm.

# FRIED BANANAS

SERVES 4-6

Fried bananas are often served in Brasil as an accompaniment to grilled meat – try them with Chilli & Cumin Marinated Hanger Steak (page 56). Traditionally, a semi-sweet banana variety such as *banana prata* (silver banana) is used, but you can substitute slightly under-ripe bananas, or even plantains.

60g plain flour
2 eggs
50g fresh breadcrumbs
50g panko breadcrumbs
4–6 firm, slightly under-ripe bananas
vegetable or groundnut oil, for frying
sea salt

★ ★ ★ ★ ★ ★ ★ ★ ★ ★ ★ ★ ★ ★ ★ ★ ★ ★ ★ ★

Mix the flour with a pinch of salt in a shallow bowl. Lightly beat the eggs in a separate bowl and mix together the two types of breadcrumbs in a third bowl.

Peel the bananas and halve them lengthways. Coat the banana halves evenly with the seasoned flour, egg and breadcrumbs. Set aside.

Heat enough oil to shallow fry the bananas in a wide, shallow pan. (If using a deep-fat fryer, heat the oil to 180°C/350°F.) When the oil is hot, add the bananas in batches and cook for about 2 minutes on each side, until golden brown. Remove and drain on kitchen paper. Transfer to a warmed plate and serve immediately.

# SWEET POTATO
FRIES

SERVES 4

These fries are one of the most popular dishes at Cabana. The sweet potatoes turn a wonderful bright orange when fried, and are complemented by the deep red paprika, which adds a subtle spice.

500g (about 2 large) sweet potatoes
vegetable oil, for deep-fat frying
1 tsp smoked paprika
sea salt

★ ★ ★ ★ ★ ★ ★ ★ ★ ★ ★ ★ ★ ★ ★ ★ ★ ★ ★ ·

Cut the potatoes lengthways into 1cm thick chips. Heat the oil in a medium pan or deep-fat fryer to 130°C/265°F. Fry the potatoes in small batches for 3–4 minutes, until soft and tender but not browned. Remove and drain on kitchen paper. Set aside at room temperature.

When you are ready to eat, heat the oil to 180°C/350°F. Carefully add a batch of par-cooked chips to the hot oil and cook for 2–4 minutes, until golden brown and crisp. If not using a deep-fat fryer, you may need to adjust the heat if the chips brown too quickly. Remove and drain on kitchen paper. While hot, sprinkle with a little smoked paprika and sea salt. Keep warm while frying the rest of the chips. Transfer to 1 large or individual warmed bowls and serve immediately.

# HOW TO SAMBA

Samba is the beat of Brasil and the heart of Carnaval, Brasil's biggest and most famous festival. The dance has African origins, and is characterized by sensual hip movements and the flirtatious passion of the dance partners. The dance is so integral to Brasil that most cities have their own *sambadromo*, a specially built exhibition space for the local samba schools to perform and compete in.

Here are the basic samba moves for you to try. The rhythm is '1-and-2, 3-and-4'. Practise it slowly to begin with, then you can gradually build up speed.

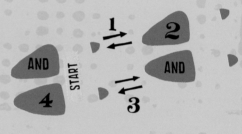

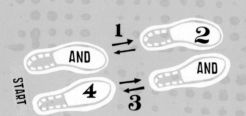

## MAN

## WOMAN

Step forward with your left foot (count 1)

Move your right foot to your left foot (and)

Left foot in place, weight shifts to it (count 2)

Step backward with your right foot (count 3)

Move your left foot to your right foot (and)

Right foot in place, weight shifts to it (count 4)

Step backward with your right foot (count 1)

Move your left foot to your right foot (and)

Right foot in place, weight shifts to it (count 2)

Step forward with your left foot (count 3)

Move your right foot to your left foot (and)

Left foot in place, weight shifts to it (count 4)

Now you have the moves, try out your footwork
with the top ten tracks on the Cabana jukebox:

## MAS QUE NADA
Sérgio Mendes feat. The Black Eyed Peas
★ ★ ★ ★

## SUN IS SHINING
Bebel Gilberto
★ ★ ★ ★

## NOVA BOSSA NOVA
Marcos Valle
★ ★ ★ ★

## GHOST TOWN
Veep
★ ★ ★ ★

## MENINHA
Nu Braz
★ ★ ★ ★

## CALIFORNIAN SOUL
Wilson das Neves
★ ★ ★ ★

## EMORIO
Sérgio Mendes
★ ★ ★ ★

## SUMMERTIME
Rosinha de Valença
★ ★ ★ ★

## BRASILIAN LOVE SONG
Nat King Cole
★ ★ ★ ★

## TAKE ME BACK TO PIAUI
Juca Chaves

# SWEET
# &
# REFRESHING

# AVOCADO ICE CREAM

**MAKES ABOUT 1.2 LITRES
(SERVES 10–12)**

Avocado is eaten as a fruit in Brasil, so don't be surprised if you see it popping up on dessert menus. It's popular in mousses, but we like it best in ice cream, as its richness results in a wonderfully smooth texture. It might sound odd at first, but do give this a go – it's truly delicious.

250g caster sugar
zest and juice of 2 lemons
zest and juice of 2 limes
200ml double cream
600ml whole milk
4 large ripe avocados
pinch of fine sea salt

★ ★ ★ ★ ★ ★ ★ ★ ★ ★ ★ ★ ★ ★ ★ ★ ★ ★

Put the sugar and lemon and lime zest and juice in a heavy-based saucepan. Slowly bring to the boil, stirring to dissolve the sugar. Once the sugar has melted, add the cream and stir well. Gradually bring to the boil. As soon as it starts to bubble up, remove the pan from the heat and pour in the milk. Halve the avocados, then remove the stones, scoop out the flesh and place in a food processor or blender. Pour in the milk and cream mixture and blitz until smooth, scraping the sides to make sure there are no chunks of avocado left.

Pour the mixture into the bowl of an ice-cream machine and churn until almost set (or according to the manufacturer's instructions). Transfer to a clean plastic container and freeze for at least a few hours until firm. (If you do not have an ice-cream maker, freeze the mixture in a shallow plastic container. Take it out after a couple of hours and whisk it by hand or with an electric whisk. Repeat the process twice, then return the ice cream to the freezer for a final freeze.)

# COCONUT & LIME SORBET

MAKES ABOUT 1 LITRE (SERVES 6–8)

This refreshing sorbet is perfect for a hot day. The lime's tartness cuts through the coconut cream to create a tangy treat that will give you dreams of suntan lotion and palm trees.

300g caster sugar
juice of 3 and finely grated zest of 4 limes
750ml coconut cream

Put a large freezerproof bowl in the freezer. Put the sugar, lime juice and 250ml coconut cream in a saucepan, place over a high heat and stir to encourage the sugar to dissolve. Bring to a simmer and cook for about 5 minutes, until thickened slightly. Remove from the heat and stir in the remaining coconut cream. Pour the mixture through a fine sieve into the chilled bowl, pressing through any lumps of coconut cream, then add the lime zest.

Pour the mixture into an ice-cream maker and churn until you get a soft sorbet consistency. Transfer to a clean plastic container and freeze for a few hours until the sorbet is firm. (If you do not have an ice-cream maker, freeze the mixture in a shallow plastic container. Take it out after a couple of hours and whisk it by hand or with an electric whisk. Repeat the process twice, then return the sorbet to the freezer for a final freeze.)

To make it easier to scoop, put the sorbet in the fridge for 30 minutes to allow it to soften slightly before serving.

# DRINKS TIPS & TRICKS

## VANILLA SUGAR

You can buy vanilla sugar in supermarkets, but it's really easy to make it yourself: just put a couple of lightly bruised or scraped-out vanilla pods in a jar of sugar and leave to infuse for a few days.

## CRACKED ICE

The weather is so hot in Brasil that crushed ice melts too quickly, so it's traditional to use cracked ice instead. For a truly authentic cocktail, you can make cracked ice by placing a handful of ice cubes in a clean plastic bag and bashing them into chunks using a rolling pin. You could also use a pestle and mortar or an ice cracker (see page 100).

## GOMME SYRUP & SIMPLE SYRUP

Gomme syrup is a sweetener that's often used in bars and restaurants to make alcoholic cocktails, as it gives drinks a silky texture. At home, it can easily be substituted with a simple sugar syrup made from equal quantities of sugar and water heated over a medium heat until the sugar has dissolved.

## STRAWBERRY PURÉE

To make your own strawberry purée, whizz a punnet of hulled and roughly chopped strawberries in a small blender. You can freeze it in an ice cube tray and use it when needed to make cocktails and smoothies.

# AMAZON ICED TEA

SERVES 2

With a climate that rarely dips below 20°C, it's no wonder that iced tea is a popular thirst-quencher in Brasil. There, it's often home-made with *mate*, a South American tea made from the leaves of the *erva-mate* plant. Green tea makes a great substitute.

100ml green tea, infused overnight and strained
200ml apple juice
50ml elderflower cordial
50ml lime juice
a few mint leaves
handful of ice cubes

Put all the ingredients in a cocktail shaker and shake vigorously for a few minutes. Strain into chilled tall glasses or tumblers and top up with ice cubes. Serve immediately.

 # LIMONADA SUISSA

SERVES 1

At the turn of the nineteenth century, Swiss chocolatiers came to Brasil to make chocolate due to the abundance of cacao trees. They created this refreshing drink to cool them down in the hot climate.

½ lemon
½ lime
1 tbsp caster sugar, or to taste
handful of ice cubes
about 175ml soda water

★ ★ ★ ★ ★ ★ ★ ★ ★ ★ ★ ★ ★ ★ ★ ★ ★ ★

Cut the lemon and lime into small wedges and place them in a sturdy glass or tumbler. Add the sugar and muddle the ingredients until the sugar has dissolved. Fill the glass two-thirds full with ice, then top with soda water. Stir well and serve immediately.

# BANANA BERRY REFRESCO

SERVES 1

Bacana means 'cool' in Portuguese, and this berry soda is not only refreshing, but is also easy to make, and looks beautiful in a clear glass garnished with fresh fruit. A *refresco* is a cold fruit drink that's sipped as an alternative to a *refrigerante* (a bottled or canned soft drink).

4 blackberries, plus extra to garnish (optional)
4 raspberries, plus extra to garnish (optional)
½ tsp vanilla sugar (page 96)
handful of cracked ice (page 96)
2 tbsp grapefruit juice
100ml lemonade
50ml soda water

Muddle the berries with the vanilla sugar in a tall, sturdy glass, then fill with cracked ice until it is two-thirds full. Add the grapefruit juice and stir. Top with the lemonade and soda. Stir again and serve immediately, garnished with blackberries and raspberries if you like.

LIMONADA
SUISSA

BANANA
BERRY
REFRESCO

AMAZON
ICED TEA

KEY TO PICTURE OPPOSITE

# YOUR CAIPIRINHA KIT

Fancy becoming a caipirinha master? Here are the tools you'll need to perfect your skills.

 **A SHOT MEASURER**

Because you can have too much of a good thing.

 **A SMALL SERRATED KNIFE**

To slice your limes thinly.

 **A SMALL WOODEN CHOPPING BOARD**

For only the finest lime chopping.

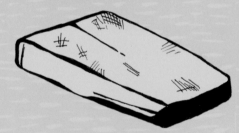

 **AN ICE CRACKER**

Ice for a caipirinha should be in rough chunks rather than crushed. Use an ice cracker or a rolling pin as described on page 96. If you can't find one, use a long metal spoon to crack your ice cubes into pieces.

 **A DURABLE BASE FOR MUDDLING**

So you won't ruin your caipirinha by breaking the glass through over-vigorous muddling.

 **A WOODEN MUDDLER**

To muddle your limes and sugar perfectly.

# CAIPIRINHA GRANITA

MAKES ABOUT 600ML (SERVES 6)

As you may have noticed, we're rather partial to a caipirinha, whether it's in a glass, on a roast chicken (page 40), or in a granita. Alcohol can be tricky because it freezes at a lower temperature than water, so this is the best way to enjoy a frozen caipirinha. And the best part is that it's dead simple to do.

100g caster sugar
100ml fresh lime juice (2½ large limes)
200ml cachaça
freshly grated lime zest, to serve
cachaça, to serve

★ ★ ★ ★ ★ ★ ★ ★ ★ ★ ★ ★ ★ ★ ★ ★ ★ ★ ★

Put 200ml water and the sugar in a saucepan and stir over a high heat until the sugar has dissolved. Stop stirring and leave the syrup to simmer for a few minutes to thicken slightly. Remove the pan from the heat and add the lime juice and cachaça. Pour the mixture into a metal tray or a wide plastic container (with lid) and leave to cool completely.

Cover the tray with clingfilm and freeze for a few hours, until the mixture is frozen around the edges and slushy in the middle. Use a fork to break up the ice into smaller crystals. Return the tray to the freezer. Repeat this process 3 more times every ½–1 hour until the mixture is completely frozen and has the texture of snow.

When ready to serve, roughly fork up the granita, then spoon into chilled serving glasses. Sprinkle with a little lime zest and add a shot of cachaça, if you like.

# THE PERFECT CAIPIRINHA

SERVES 1

The *caipirinha*, which means 'little country girl' in Portuguese, is Brasil's national cocktail. There are many stories about how it was invented, but this is our favourite: in the olden days, people would press a cloth moistened with alcohol to their heads to reduce a fever and suck a lime to improve their immunity. One day, a feverish man found the alcohol on his forehead dripping into his mouth as he sucked a lime, and since it was bitter he ate a spoonful of sugar. He got better, and the caipirinha was born. You can use ordinary white or granulated sugar, but we like the slightly caramelized flavour of golden caster sugar. There are as many variations of fruit caipirinhas as there are fruit, but opposite are three of our favourites. Try experimenting to see what creations you can concoct.

1½ limes, skin on, cut into rough cubes
1 tbsp golden caster sugar
65ml cachaça (we like Velho Barreiro)
handful of cracked ice (see page 96)

★ ★ ★ ★ ★ ★ ★ ★ ★ ★ ★ ★ ★ ★ ★ ★ ★ ★ ★

Put the limes and sugar in a sturdy glass tumbler. Muddle them with a cocktail muddler or the end of a small rolling pin to extract the juice from the lime and dissolve the sugar. Add the cachaça and cracked ice and give it a stir. Finally, top the glass with more cracked ice and add a wooden lollipop stick for stirring. Serve immediately.

# VARIATIONS

## STRAWBERRY & LIME CAIPIRINHA

Add 3-4 strawberries to the limes before muddling, then proceed as opposite.

## PINEAPPLE & MINT CAIPIRINHA

Replace the limes with 2 shredded mint leaves and 5 cubes of ripe pineapple, then proceed as opposite. Garnish with extra mint.

## PASSION FRUIT CAIPIRINHA

Replace the limes with the pulp of a passion fruit. Proceed as opposite and garnish with half a passion fruit.

# CACHAÇA:

# DRINK IT, OR RUN YOUR CAR ON IT

Say it with us now: cachaça. *Ka-sha-sa*. It's the national drink of Brasil and the base of its best-known cocktail. Like rum, it's a sugar cane spirit, but unlike rum it's distilled directly from fermented sugar cane juice, rather than from the molasses (the syrupy by-product that's created when sugar cane is turned into sugar).

Also like rum, cachaça comes in a variety of styles and characters, from the un-aged spirit to the more sophisticated, matured, artisanal product. The common 'white' cachaça was originally considered only a poor man's drink, no better than hooch. It is often given the slang name *pinga* (from the Portuguese *pingar*, to drip, referring to the distillation process), and is a clear, strong spirit with a grassy flavour that's perfect for mixing and cocktails. However, there has recently been a surge in the production of mature cachaça, which is aged in wooden barrels, is darker in colour and has more mellow flavours, such as cinnamon, vanilla and dried fruits. This can be sipped on its own and makes a great alternative to an after-dinner brandy or whisky.

A short time ago it would have been hard to get your hands on a bottle of cachaça unless you'd conveniently been on a trip to Brasil or Portugal. However, now that the spirit is gaining popularity, it should be simple to find brands such as Sagatiba, especially in larger supermarkets. If you're at a loss or simply don't like the taste of cachaça (some people can find it too rough or strong), you can always substitute vodka or rum – we won't tell!

Oh, and Brasilians really do sometimes run their cars on it. If you're ever crossing the road in Brasil and notice a waft of sweetness in the air, that's the ethanol from sugar cane. That probably isn't one to try at home...

# RIO 2014

Rio 2014 is our tribute to the World Cup, and our take on Sangria: a red wine punch with an added slug of cachaça. It's great for sharing and for celebrating with, so enjoy it with friends over a long evening in the sun.

ice cubes
150ml cachaça
225ml orange juice
110ml lemon juice
100ml simple sugar syrup (page 96)
225ml red wine
1 orange, sliced
1 lemon, sliced
small handful of mint leaves

★ ★ ★ ★ ★ ★ ★ ★ ★ ★ ★ ★ ★ ★ ★ ★ ★ ★ ★ ★

Fill a large jug with ice cubes, then add the cachaça, orange and lemon juice and sugar syrup. Give the mixture a stir, then pour in the red wine. If you like, pour the red wine over the back of a tablespoon to create distinct layers within the jug. Garnish with the orange and lemon slices and mint leaves and serve immediately.

# FROZEN CLASSIC CAIPIRINHA

Inspired by summer days on Rio's Ipanema beach, we created this retro frozen cocktail as a fun twist on Brasil's most famous drink. Enjoy a slurp of the tart, refreshing classic version, or add fresh fruit or purees to create your own concoctions.

70ml cachaça
80ml lime juice
50ml gomme or simple sugar syrup (page 96)
plenty of cracked ice (page 96)
2 thin slices of lime, to garnish

★ ★ ★ ★ ★ ★ ★ ★ ★ ★ ★ ★ ★ ★ ★ ★ ★ ★ ★

Put all the ingredients except the slices of lime in a blender. Blend on high until completely smooth – this could take up to 6 minutes. For the ultimate effect, pour into martini glasses (although any glass will do), and garnish with a slice of lime.

*All three cocktails photographed on pages 112–113.

# CARMEN MIRANDA

SERVES 2

Carmen Miranda was a Portuguese-born Brasilian samba singer, dancer, Broadway actress and film star who rose to fame in the 1940s. This spicy, fruity cocktail is a tribute to her passionate nature (and of course her iconic tropical fruit headdress!).

½ red chilli, deseeded and finely chopped
120ml mango purée
70ml spiced rum (we like Rebellion)
30ml lime juice
10ml vanilla syrup, made from simple sugar syrup (page 96) flavoured with vanilla sugar or plain sugar and a little vanilla extract
4 thin slices of red chilli, to garnish
handful of ice cubes

Muddle the chopped chilli in the bottom of a cocktail shaker with a cocktail muddler or the end of a small rolling pin. Add the mango purée, rum, lime juice and vanilla syrup along with a handful of ice cubes. Cover the cocktail shaker and shake vigorously for a few seconds. Pour short tumblers filled with ice, then garnish with a couple of chilli slices.

 # BRASILITO: THE BRASILIAN MOJITO

SERVES 1

The Brasilito ('Little Brasilian') is an adaptation of the El Draque ('The Dragon'), a direct ancestor of the popular mojito we know today. Legend has it that the El Draque was invented by the pirate Richard Drake in honour of his captain Sir Francis Drake, who was nicknamed *El Draque* by the Spanish and Portuguese of his crew. Our version uses brown sugar and aged cachaça to give a richer flavour, but you can easily replace these with white sugar and un-aged cachaça if they are easier to find.

1½ limes, cut into rough cubes
2 tsp brown sugar
small handful mint leaves
handful of cracked ice (page 96)
35ml gold cachaça (we like Velho Barreiro)
25ml gomme or simple syrup (page 96)

Put the limes and sugar in a tall glass. Muddle them with a cocktail muddler or the end of a small rolling pin to extract the juice from the lime and dissolve the sugar. Add the mint leaves and gently muddle with the back of a spoon. Fill the glass two-thirds full with cracked ice, then add the remaining ingredients and vigorously mix with a spoon. Top with cracked ice and garnish with an extra spring of mint.

# BLOODY MARIA

Our take on a Bloody Mary uses cachaça as the alcohol base, and features Cabana's own Bloody Maria mix, which includes Tabasco, mustard and horseradish for extra kick.

½ lime
1 tsp caster sugar, or to taste
handful of crushed ice
35ml cachaça
25ml Bloody Maria mix (below)
50ml tomato juice

Cut the lime into 4 wedges, leaving the skins on. Place in a tall, sturdy glass with the sugar. Muddle them with a cocktail muddler or the end of a small rolling pin to extract the juice from the lime and dissolve the sugar. Fill the glass half full with crushed ice, then stir in the cachaça and Bloody Maria mix. Fill to the top with tomato juice and a little more crushed ice, if you like. Stir well and serve immediately.

 # BLOODY MARIA MIX

MAKES ABOUT 175ML (7 SERVINGS)

145ml Worcestershire sauce
1 tsp creamed horseradish
2 tsp Tabasco
½ tsp finely ground mixed peppercorns
1 tsp celery salt
½ tsp sea salt
1 garlic clove, finely crushed
1 tsp English mustard
1 tsp balsamic vinegar

Mix all the ingredients together in a small jar with a lid and keep chilled until ready to use. The mixture keeps well in the fridge for a few days.

# WATERMELON MARTINI

SERVES 1

Lizzy drank this at Bar Astor in Ipanema on her first night in Rio, and instantly knew she was in Brasil. When we got home we were determined to recreate it, and here's the result: the flavour of hot summer nights.

5 small chunks fresh, ripe watermelon (skin removed), plus extra to garnish
35ml vodka
15ml cloudy apple juice
10ml passion fruit liqueur (or substitute vodka)
10ml watermelon syrup or simple sugar syrup (page 96), plus extra for drizzling
handful of ice cubes

★ ★ ★ ★ ★ ★ ★ ★ ★ ★ ★ ★ ★ ★ ★ ★ ★ ★ ★

Place a martini glass in the freezer for 20 minutes to get it well chilled and frosty. Muddle the watermelon in the bottom of a cocktail shaker with a cocktail muddler or the end of a small rolling pin, leaving in any pips. Add the remaining ingredients with a handful of ice cubes, then cover the cocktail shaker and shake vigorously for a few seconds. Double-strain it into the chilled glass, making sure there are no pips.

Garnish with a slice of watermelon or 3 small watermelon balls on a cocktail stick. If you have watermelon syrup to hand, drizzle a little over the watermelon garnish, then serve immediately.

# STRAWBERRY BATIDA

**SERVES 2**

The *batida* is another classic Brasilian cocktail. It literally means 'shaken', and it's a bit like an alcoholic milkshake: lighter than a caipirinha and thickened with coconut milk. You can make it in advance and keep it in the fridge until ready to serve.

130ml cachaça
100g hulled strawberries, plus extra to garnish
50ml coconut cream
juice of 1 lime
4 tsp caster sugar
handful of ice cubes

★ ★ ★ ★ ★ ★ ★ ★ ★ ★ ★ ★ ★ ★ ★ ★ ★ ★

Place 2 glasses in the freezer to chill. Put all the ingredients (except the strawberries to garnish) in a blender with a handful of ice cubes. Blend at medium speed until smooth, then pour into the chilled glasses. Garnish each glass with a fresh strawberry and serve immediately.

STRAWBERRY BATIDA

WATERMELON MARTINI

BLOODY MARIA

KEY TO PICTURE OPPOSITE

# CABANA COLADA

SERVES 2

This is our version of a piña colada, and uses cachaça and lots of lime for a citrus kick. For a virgin Cabana Colada, which is also very good, just leave out the cachaça.

2 tbsp coconut cream
2 tbsp lemon juice
2 tbsp simple sugar syrup (page 96)
4 tbsp pineapple juice
110ml coconut water
35ml cachaça
large handful of ice cubes
sprigs of mint, to garnish

Place 2 tall glasses in the freezer to chill. Put all the ingredients except the mint in a blender with a large handful of ice cubes. Blend well to a smooth, silky consistency. Pour into the chilled glasses, garnish with the mint sprigs and serve.

 # LYCHEE SAKENINHA

SERVES 1

This is one of the most popular cocktails in the clubs of São Paulo, which has the largest Japanese community in the country, and therefore a ready supply of sake. It's made the same way as a caipirinha, but uses sake instead of cachaça, and lychees for a sweet, perfumed flavour.

5 tinned lychees, drained, plus extra
    to garnish
2–4 tbsp lychee syrup from the tin, to taste
120ml sake
handful of cracked ice (page 96)

Muddle the lychees and lychee syrup with a cocktail muddler or the end of a small rolling pin in a tall, sturdy glass. Add sake and cracked ice. Give it a quick stir, then garnish with a lychee. Serve immediately.

# BRASILIAN STREET FOOD PARTY

Take your friends on a trip to a São Paulo street market with this fun twist on a drinks and canapé party. There are plenty of things you can make ahead so that you're not stuck in the kitchen when all the fun is happening outside. To serve 8–10, you'll need to double the quantities of the Sweetcorn Soup Shots and Chicken 'Espírito Santo'. The quantities of caipirinhas we'll leave to you!

## MENU

### TOASTED GIANT CORN
(PAGE 24)

### SWEETCORN SOUP SHOTS
(PAGE 25)

### PÃO DE QUEIJO
(PAGE 13)

### COXINHAS
(PAGE 12)

### BOLINHOS
(PAGE 18)
#### WITH CHILLI MAYONNAISE
(PAGE 69)

### CHICKEN 'ESPÍRITO SANTO'
#### WITH TOMATO & PEANUT SAUCE
(PAGE 32)

### AVOCADO ICE CREAM
(PAGE 92)

### DIY CAIPIRINHAS
(PAGE 104)

## WITH THE INVITATIONS

✚ Ask guests to bring along their favourite fruit to experiment with DIY caipirinhas in an assortment of fruit flavours.

## THE DAY BEFORE

- Make the Toasted Giant Corn and store in an airtight container.
- Make the Sweetcorn Soup and set aside in the fridge.
- Make the Avocado Ice Cream and store in an airtight container in the freezer.
- Prepare the Coxinhas and Bolinhos, then refrigerate, ready to deep-fry the next day.
- Make the Tomato & Peanut Sauce and Chilli Mayonnaise and set aside in the fridge.

## FOUR HOURS BEFORE GUESTS ARRIVE

- Make the Pão de Queijo and chill, ready to bake.
- Prepare the Chicken 'Espírito Santo' skewers, cover and refrigerate.
- Make the Molho Vinagrete for the Sweetcorn Soup Shots.

## ONE HOUR BEFORE GUESTS ARRIVE

- Deep-fry the Coxinhas and Bolinhos and keep warm, covered, in a low oven.

## HALF AN HOUR BEFORE GUESTS ARRIVE

- Set up a caipirinha bar with all the ingredients for Classic Caipirinhas, a few varieties of fruits and a set of instructions for guests to make their own caipirinhas.
- Bake the Pão de Queijo and keep warm in the oven.
- Pour the toasted corn into small bowls and arrange around the room for snacking.

## WHEN GUESTS ARRIVE

- Encourage guests to make their own caipirinhas, adding their favourite fruit to the selection.
- Reheat the Sweetcorn Soup and serve in espresso cups with garnishes.
- Bake the Chicken 'Espírito Santo' skewers and reheat the Tomato & Peanut Sauce.
- Serve some canapés every five minutes or so.
- Remove the ice cream from the freezer around 10 minutes before you're ready to serve it to give it time to soften. Serve scoops in small bowls or glasses, with dessertspoons.

# COCO CABANA

SERVES 4

Drink this and you'll be instantly transported to Copacabana beach. The combination of rum, cachaça, strawberries and coconut can't help but give you that holiday feeling, even if you're in rainy England in July.

75ml cachaça
75ml Malibu
50ml coconut cream
50ml lemon juice
50ml simple sugar syrup (page 96)
90ml pineapple juice
180ml coconut water
75ml strawberry purée (page 96)
ice cubes
1 lemon, sliced
1 orange, sliced

Pour all the ingredients except the orange and lemon slices into a large jug and stir well. Fill with ice and stir again. Top with lemon and orange slices.

# INDEX

# CABANA – HOW IT ALL BEGAN

★ ★ ★ ★ ★ ★ ★ ★ ★ ★ ★ ★ ★ ★ ★ ★ ★ ★ ★ ★ ★ ★ ★ ★ ★ ★

It all started with a phone call. Jamie Barber had always been captivated by *churrascarias*, or Brasilian barbecue restaurants: the ballet of waiters gliding around tables, huge skewers of freshly cooked meat, bright colours, zingy flavours and the smoke of the barbecue pit. This was always the image in his mind's eye, but when he visited them in London he found them disappointing.

He called up David Ponté, a fellow restaurateur and old friend, in February 2011 and made a simple proposition: 'What about doing Brasilian barbecue – but doing it properly?' David was born in Rio, and a childhood in the country and subsequent trips back home had always left him with a deep *saudade* – a longing and nostalgia for his memories of home. Jamie didn't have to ask him twice.

Together, they set out to create a Brasilian barbecue restaurant that would showcase the best of Brasil: the optimism, the vibrant ingredients, the spice. There would be no football, no beach bums and no girl from Ipanema. Jamie's sister Lizzy hopped aboard to whip the boys into shape, Chef Director David Rood set to work creating and testing recipes from a constant stream of ideas – and Cabana was born.